DOING YOUR EARLY YEARS RESEARCH PROJECT

Sara Miller McCune founded SAGE Publishing in 1965 to support
the dissemination of usable knowledge and educate a global
community. SAGE publishes more than 1000 journals and over
800 new books each year, spanning a wide range of subject areas.
Our growing selection of library products includes archives, data,
case studies and video. SAGE remains majority owned by our
founder and after her lifetime will become owned by a charitable
trust that secures the company's continued independence.

Los Angeles | London | New Delhi | Singapore | Washington DC | Melbourne

4TH Edition

DOING YOUR EARLY YEARS RESEARCH PROJECT

A STEP-BY-STEP GUIDE

GUY ROBERTS-HOLMES

Los Angeles | London | New Delhi
Singapore | Washington DC | Melbourne

Los Angeles | London | New Delhi
Singapore | Washington DC | Melbourne

SAGE Publications Ltd
1 Oliver's Yard
55 City Road
London EC1Y 1SP

SAGE Publications Inc.
2455 Teller Road
Thousand Oaks, California 91320

SAGE Publications India Pvt Ltd
B 1/I 1 Mohan Cooperative Industrial Area
Mathura Road
New Delhi 110 044

SAGE Publications Asia-Pacific Pte Ltd
3 Church Street
#10-04 Samsung Hub
Singapore 049483

Editor: Jude Bowen
Assistant editor: Catriona McMullen
Assistant editor, digital: Chloe Statham
Production editor: Nicola Carrier
Copyeditor: Sharon Cawood
Proofreader: Thea Watson
Indexer: Cathy Heath
Marketing manager: Lorna Patkai
Cover design: Wendy Scott
Typeset by: C&M Digitals (P) Ltd, Chennai, India
Printed in the UK

Library of Congress Control Number: 2017953115

British Library Cataloguing in Publication data

A catalogue record for this book is available from
the British Library

ISBN 978-1-52642-424-2
ISBN 978-1-52642-425-9 (pbk)

This book is dedicated to my dear brother, Paul 'Pablo' Christopher Roberts-Holmes (02/08/64 to 05/02/01). Paul's love, warmth, humour and passion for life are greatly missed by all who knew him.

CONTENTS

ABOUT THE AUTHOR

Dr Guy Roberts-Holmes is an Associate Professor in the The Helen Hamlyn Centre for Pedagogy (0–11 years) at UCL, Institute of Education. His recent research has focused upon the role of numerical data in early years education. He has researched the introduction of the revised EYFS (DfE, 2012) and the Introduction of Reception Baseline Assessment (NUT and ATL, 2015) which won the BERA Impact Award (2016). He has recently researched Ability Labelling in the Early Years and KS1 (NEU, 2017). His latest book (with Alice Bradbury) is called *The Datafication of Primary and Early Years Education Playing with Numbers* (2017).

ACKNOWLEDGEMENTS

For Pamela and her continued love, inspiration and creativity.

Thank you to the Canterbury Christ Church University Early Childhood Studies students who shared their research projects with me: Shelley Angel, Lisa Burnap, Gemma Cook, Stephanie Dennehy, Katherine Gough, Martyn Kitney, Eleanor MacDonald, and Georgina Moxon. More recently, thank you to the University College London Institute of Education, MA Early Years Education students Anthony Leete, Eleanor Rea and Michelle Palser whose dissertations are inspirational.

The author and publisher are grateful for permission to reproduce the following material in this book:

Figure 1.2 – Blaxter, L, Hughes, C. and Tight, M. (2010) How to Research, 4th Edition, Open University Press/ McGraw-Hill Education. Copyright © Blaxter, L, Hughes, C. and Tight, M 2010. Reproduced by permission of The McGraw-Hill Companies, Inc.

Figure 5.6 from P. Clough and C. Nutbrown (2007), *A Student's Guide to Methodology*, Sage Publications: London. Reprinted with permission.

Figure 6.1 from Clark, A. (2017) *Listening to Young Children: a guide to understanding and using the Mosaic approach*, 3rd Edition, London: Jessica Kingsley Publishers for National Children's Bureau. Copyright © Alison Clark 2017. Foreword copyright © Peter Moss 2017. Reproduced with permission of the Licensor through PLS Clear.

Chapter 6, poem from Edwards, C., Gandini, L. and Forman, G., *The Hundred Languages of Children: The Reggio Emilia Approach to Early Childhood Education*. From the Catalogue of the Exhibition 'The Hundred Languages of Children', © Preschools and Infant-toddler Centers – Instituzione of the Municipality of Reggio Emilia, Italy, published by Reggio Children, 1996.

Reggio Children/Centro Internazionale Loris Malaguzzi, Via Bligny, 1/a 42124 Reggio Emilia, http://zerosei.comune.re.it/

English translation by Lella Gandini Ó Lella Gandini, 1983. First published in English in *The Hundred Languages of Children: The Reggio Emilia Approach to Early Childhood Education*, 1st edition, edited by Carolyn Edwards, Lella Gandini and George Forman, 1993, and *The Hundred Languages of Children: The Reggio Emilia Approach, Advanced Reflections*, 2nd edition, 1998, Ablex Publishing. Ó Carolyn Edwards, Lella Gandini and George Forman, 1993, 1998. Reproduced with the permission of Greenwood Publishing Group, Inc., Westport, CT.

Chapter 6, excerpt from 'I Forgot the Sky!' Children's Stories Contained Within Their Drawings, Coates, E., *International Journal of Early Years Education* (2002: Taylor & Francis), reprinted by permission of the publisher (Taylor & Francis Ltd, http://www.tandfonline.com).

Figures 7.2, and 7.3 from Y. P. Lancaster and P. Kirby (2010), *Listening to Young Children (2nd Edition)*, Open University Press/McGraw-Hill Education. Copyright © Y. Penny Lancaster, and reproduced with the kind permission of Open International Publishing Ltd. All rights reserved.

Table 11.4 from D. Wyse & K. Cowan (2017), *The Good Writing Guide for Education Students* (4th Edition), Sage Publications: London. Reprinted with permission.

FOREWORD

Research can often seem a lonely business. The initial thinking about the need for enquiry, the creation of resources and relationships to enable research to take place, along with sustaining its implementation, can seem overwhelming. This can be as true for the experienced researcher as it is for the novice. *Doing Your Early Years Research Project* is a perfect companion. It brings many voices, structures and examples to support and challenge the researcher.

The text can be approached as a narrative of research – taking the reader-researcher through each stage from a developmental perspective. This starts with the building blocks of research: from considerations of what it means to take on the role and identity of a researcher to the creation of questions and aims that will fuel the enquiry. Within the text, there are carefully interwoven examples from many individuals' experiences alongside structured activities to offer the reader guidance and helpful conversation at each stage. The journey continues through a consideration of ethics, methodology, the conduct of specific data collection methods and the analysis of data. Each chapter provides a combination of scaffolding for learning about ideas and practices alongside grounded illustrations of actual experiences. These provide an excellent dialogic accompaniment and create a balance of support and critical challenge for the start of research.

The book also addresses ideas and issues that run beneath its approach to the development of the individual as an excellent *researcher* and the conduct of first-rate *research*. These include articulate and lively engagement with considerations that must connect with any research with children: the position of young children in society; policy contexts; social exclusion and social justice; power relations and child rights. The reader is enabled to bring their research into contact with debates about how best to form socially inclusive relationships with children, how recent thinking in ethics is reflected in new ideas and practices about young children, and consent and discoveries about the benefits and obstacles of using new media in enquiry. Meaning making is key to much of the book's ideas about positive change and research with young children. The ways in which adults and children create transformative connections between their lives and research are held up and examined. From creative listening to observation, from developing interviews to using images and play, the reader is given access to clear thinking and international perspectives about barriers, possibilities and new insights.

The impressive achievement of this book is to offer access to essential and basic theory and practice, whilst deepening understanding and developing a sophisticated critical framework to support high quality research.

The book is relevant to the practitioner and to the early years student, whilst offering insights to the more experienced researcher. Dr Roberts-Holmes makes enquiry alive and accessible and his text will inspire the reader to see how their research can benefit young children and those who live and work with them.

Professor Phil Jones, Department of Early Years and Primary Education,
Institute of Education, University of London

GLOSSARY

Action research   Action research or practitioner research attempts to instigate change in the form of improved practice, policy and culture within an institution. Action research is a collaborative and participatory research approach.

Analysis   The process of thinking deeply about your collected data and discussing, interpreting and explaining it in order to answer your research questions.

Article 12   Article 12 of the United Nations *Convention on the Rights of the Child* (UN, 1989) declares that children have the right to hold an opinion about issues concerning them. Article 12 encourages early childhood researchers to engage children in research that affects them and to listen and act on what children say.

Assent   A legal term referring to agreement by children to participate in your research. Legally, this consent is known as assent rather than consent because legally children have no right to give informed consent because they are too young. It is generally considered by early childhood researchers not to be a useful term.

Case study   Useful for finding out more about the detailed, subtle and complex social interactions and processes operating within a narrowly defined context such as a single early childhood centre or family.

Child-centred methodology   The ethical values and principles which place children centre stage throughout the research process, for example the Mosaic approach.

Code   The process of classifying, marking or identifying different pieces of data for later analysis.

Convenience sampling   A form of purposive sampling that enables you to opportunistically choose the early childhood setting, practitioners and children for your research.

Data   Can be either qualitative interviews or quantitative numbers and are collected by research methods. The data are analysed and written about using literature.

Documentation   A range of evidence collected by and with young children about their early childhood institution. Documentation in the form of children's, practitioners' and parents' photographs, drawings, consultations and observations can be built up to provide a mosaic of perspectives on the early childhood institution.

Ethics   Ethical research involves showing respect and sensitivity towards the feelings and rights of *all* those participating in your research project. Ethical researchers carefully reflect on any unintended harm that they may cause to the participants.

Ethnography   Early childhood ethnographies aim to provide holistic accounts of the views, perspectives, beliefs and values of the children, practitioners, workers and parents in an early childhood institution.

Focus group conversations   A collaborative interview technique that is particularly effective with young children. Children may be empowered in a focus group in which they feel comfortable.

Gatekeeper   A gatekeeper decides whether or not you can proceed with your research in the institution they manage. Head teachers, early childhood centre managers and children's supervisors can all act as gatekeepers.

Generalisability   The extent to which findings from your research are true or relevant beyond your sample size and to different contexts.

Grounded theory   A systematic research approach in which theory is developed – or generated – from your research data.

Inductive analysis   The analytic approach that works from your data to the theory and is the opposite to deductive analysis.

Informed consent   Refers to the ethical principle of research participants voluntarily agreeing to participate in a research project based on the complete disclosure of all relevant information and each recipient's understanding of this. Early childhood researchers are expected to gain informed consent from all the research participants in their study. Issues of informed consent with young children hinge on whether the children competently understand what is expected of them in the research process. The general guidance is to ask parents' consent to approach children and then ask for children's consent.

Interpretivism   The belief that the social world is continually being created and constructed. Shared understandings and meanings are given to these social interactions.

Interview   On a continuum from the closed structured interview to the unstructured consultation. In order to listen respectfully to young children, early childhood researchers focus on child-centred participatory activities such as children's drawings during the consultation.

Interview guide   A set of predetermined field questions which direct the flow of the interview.

Longitudinal study   A research design that enables the researcher to look back at the research topic over time and see how different groups of people have been affected.

Methodology   Refers to the principles and values, philosophies and ideologies that underpin the entire research process. Your methodology will inform the questions that you ask, the literature you read, your methods and the analysis. Early childhood studies research is frequently driven by a child-centred methodology in which the child comes first.

Mixed methods   An approach that combines both qualitative and quantitative methods ensuring triangulation.

Objectivity Historically, researchers mistakenly believed in a neutral and disengaged researcher whose beliefs, politics and experiences did not affect the research in any way. In early childhood studies, as in other social sciences, researcher objectivity has been seen as a myth and a fallacy, hence the need for reflexivity throughout the research process.

Observation schedule An observational checklist on which specific observations concerning a targeted child or children are made.

Participant observation The researcher takes part in the activities with the participants and at the same time reflects on and researches the situation.

Pilot study Involves the researcher trialling the interview questions, the questionnaires, the observations and any form of research methods. The pilot study can alert the researcher to any potential future difficulties and the research can be appropriately amended.

Positivism The belief that the social world of people operates in a similar way to the natural physical world, and researcher subjectivity and reflexivity are not issues within the positivist tradition. The positivist tradition attempts to prove hypotheses.

Probing An interview research technique for eliciting information from the respondent.

Purposive sampling A deliberate sample of carefully selected cases that enable you to best explore your research questions in depth.

Qualitative research methods Usually involve non-numerical data collection, such as interviews, participant observation, diaries, drawings and children's photographs. Qualitative research tends to produce and analyse in-depth and detailed data. May be combined with quantitative research methods.

Quantitative research methods Usually involve numerical data collection derived from questionnaires, statistical surveys and experiments. Quantitative research tends to produce and analyse broad contextual data providing overall patterns and generalisations. May be combined with qualitative research methods.

Questionnaire A research method which enables standardised, structured and tightly organised questions to be gathered.

Random sample A representative sampling technique so that every early childhood setting, practitioner or child has an equal chance of being included in the sample and it cannot be predicted.

Reflexivity Reflexive researchers are self-aware of their biases, assumptions and interpretations of the research issues. Self-awareness of how the researcher affects the children and adults constantly informs reflexive research. Practitioner-researchers need to demonstrate self-awareness and sensitivity towards the ways in which their presence affects the data they collect and how their underlying assumptions make them interpret those data in particular ways.

Reliability A measure of research quality, so that if another researcher carried out exactly the same research as yours they would have the same findings.

Representative sampling A sampling technique such as random sampling in order to be representative of the wider group of early childhood settings, practitioners and children.

Research diary A reflective log of your thoughts and feelings as they occur during the research process. Extracts from your reflective research diary may be used in your research study when triangulated with additional pieces of data confirming your thoughts and feelings.

Research participants include all those who work with and provide material for the research project, for example colleagues, children, workers, teachers, practitioners and parents.

Reflexivity Reflexive researchers are self-aware of their biases, assumptions and interpretations of the research issues. Self-awareness of how the researcher affects the children and adults constantly informs reflexive research. Practitioner-researchers need to demonstrate self-awareness and sensitivity towards the ways in which their presence affects the data they collect and how their underlying assumptions make them interpret those data in particular ways.

Sampling How you actively and deliberately select what you are researching, for example the settings, practitioners and children. Quantitative researchers tend to use representative sampling such as random sampling as they are attempting to make their research representative. Qualitative researchers tend to use purposive sampling to explain or understand the phenomena they are studying.

Social justice Social justice research aims to make a positive contribution to the broader social good for *all* young children, their families and communities. Social justice is at the heart of politically transformative research. Fairness, justice, equality and respect are some of the principles and values underpinning social justice research.

Stratified sampling A sampling strategy that ensures that certain categories and groups and cases are included, proportionate to their numbers in the wider group.

Structured observations Focused and targeted observations such as specific child observations, event sampling and targeted running records.

Subjectivity Refers to the extent that the individual researcher's own feelings, biases and interpretations influence the research questions, data collection and interpretation. Hence, subjectivity is closely connected to reflexivity. Researcher subjectivity is sometimes used to critique researcher objectivity.

Survey Attempts to produce large volumes of broad and generalisable data using questionnaires with a large sample size. Surveys use a variety of sampling methods.

Triangulation Involves the comparison and combination of different sources of evidence in order to reach a better understanding of the research topic. Thus, the researcher's observations, interviews with participants and questionnaires all produce different pieces of evidence which can be combined and compared to give a triangulated analysis.

Unstructured observations Typically, these are in the form of reflective diary notes and anecdotal unfocused observations on the early childhood setting. When combined with triangulated evidence from practitioners, workers and parents, they can be included as data in the research report.

Validity   The interpretivist and positivist research traditions have different understandings of research validity. For the interpretivist, triangulation of participants' responses is used so that the participants' true voices are seen to be consistent and valid. For the positivist, validity is concerned with the research process and findings being replicated or copied by another researcher. The mixed methods approach tends to have good validity as it triangulates a variety of both qualitative and quantitative data collection methods.

REFERENCE

United Nations (UN) (1989) *Convention on the Rights of the Child*. New York: United Nations.

ONLINE RESOURCES

Visit **https://study.sagepub.com/roberts-holmes4e** to find a range of additional resources to aid study and support teaching.

Journal articles – a selection of scholarly journal articles support each chapter, chosen to deepen your knowledge and reinforce your learning of key topics.

Author videos – watch videos of the author discussing important chapter topics in more detail.

Useful templates – downloadable and editable templates that can be integrated into your own research project to assist with practical project milestones.

**YOU CAN
DO RESEARCH!**

LEARNING OBJECTIVES

This chapter will help you to:

- understand and demystify the process of research
- express your feelings about carrying out a research project
- understand the importance of social justice in research
- appreciate the importance of reflective practice in research
- understand the principles of high-quality research
- appreciate the everyday research skills which you already possess
- understand your own and your supervisor's responsibilities for the project.

YOUR FEELINGS ABOUT DOING RESEARCH

As you start your research project, you will probably be feeling a whole range of emotions. The following sections cover a wide variety of emotions that some students stated they felt about their forthcoming early childhood research projects. These students' positive feelings were concerned with the excitement of focusing in depth on an issue which was of real interest to them and working at their own pace and helping children. The anxieties the students had included being apprehensive about their own abilities and not having sufficient time. These positive and negative feelings about research topics are extremely common. Your early apprehension will help you generate the enthusiasm to successfully complete your research project.

As you read through the students' comments below, think about the following questions:

- Which comments do you empathise with?
- Why do you think so many students feel this way?
- How do you feel at the moment about doing your research project? Talk these feelings through with your friends and your supervisor.

I'M LOOKING FORWARD TO...

- The idea of 'digging deep' into an area that really interests me is a real energy booster.
- I'm very excited about my project as it is a topic which I'm fascinated about.
- The idea of doing research gives me 'a buzz'. It's a great opportunity to learn, to evaluate, and to evolve ideas.
- I feel that this is a good opportunity to gain further insight into an area of early childhood studies which really interests ME.
- We can choose exactly what we want to look at and I can work at my own pace.
- I want to make a change for the better and help children through my research.

ANXIETIES

- I hope I can go into sufficient depth in the area in the short timespan and do the topic the justice it deserves.
- I'm worried about not being able to get enough material together and not having the time to complete the study.
- As a single mum with three children, the amount of time I will have to spend on the project concerns me. Will I have enough?
- It feels like an enormous undertaking because I'm just not sure what I will be researching!
- I'm anxious about being out of my depth!

- I am wondering whether I am confident enough to ask professionals the questions I need answering.
- I feel I need a lot of guidance and support and hope this will be available to me.
- I am a bit wary about how to approach my area, however once I start talking to lecturers and people in the setting I feel that most of these apprehensions will disappear.
- I worry about the ethical issues.
- Am I organised enough to carry out such a project?

MYTHS ABOUT EARLY CHILDHOOD RESEARCH

The above range of feelings may arise because, for some, the very word 'research' can create anxiety. It is important to remember that research is simply a tool (MacNaughton et al., 2010), and as with any other tool, when you learn what it does, why it has been invented and how to use it, it becomes beneficial to you. This means that, because research is just a tool, you are in control of it, rather than it being in control of you. The negative associations that you may be having around the word 'research' are not unusual and can stem from commonly held myths and stereotypes. The following wrong and mistaken views about research do sometimes create emotional barriers which can then prevent early childhood practitioners from participating in the research process:

- Early childhood research can only be done by academic professors and experts.
- The research process is so intellectual, complex, mysterious and time-consuming that it cannot possibly be for people like me!
- Research produces hard facts which are unquestionable.

- Research proves things one way or the other.
- There is only one way to do research.
- Research is a strict scientific exercise.
- Research is boring.
- Research cannot change anything.
- There are no real benefits from doing research.

AN INCLUSIVE APPROACH TO EARLY CHILDHOOD RESEARCH

Below are listed some different and more inclusive viewpoints about research which many early childhood practitioners have found to be true for them:

- You already possess many 'everyday' research skills.
- Research can be done by everybody – this means you too!
- Research is simply a tool for you to use.
- Research is fun and hard work.
- Research asks questions about the things that really matter to us.
- Research can initiate personal and professional change and development.
- Research is about developing knowledge.
- Research is about discovery.
- Research is about change.
- Research helps us understand the complex issues in childhood.
- Research helps to further professionalise early childhood studies.
- Research is about questioning taken-for-granted assumptions, myths and 'commonsense' understandings.
- Research is about challenging habitual patterns of behaviour.
- Research can satisfy your fascination with an issue.
- Research can positively benefit you, your work, the children, and the setting you work in.

Which of the above statements do you agree and disagree with? To what extent do you agree with the following statement?

- Early childhood research enables us to see things about children and ourselves as practitioners in new and different ways, to challenge our habitual patterns of thinking and to possibly act in new ways.

You might be wondering what you can offer early childhood research. The good news is that early childhood is a rapidly expanding area and you can contribute to that process with your research project.

YOUR RESEARCH PROJECT WITHIN EARLY CHILDHOOD STUDIES

Although a great deal has been written about early childhood and children, there is still a lot that remains unknown concerning young children growing up in society. Today's complex society increasingly places responsibilities on early childhood practitioners to understand more about children. New legislation, policies and practice constantly change the ways in which practitioners must relate to and work with the children in their care. For example, within the UK the Early Years Foundation Stage (DfE, 2017) poses huge challenges for early years practitioners in implementing its laudable principles and aims. The EYFS has increased expectations of early childhood services and the people who work in them. There is a tremendous need to know more about the various ways in which these changing complex factors influence children and their childhoods.

Childhoods are understood as being positioned within a set of overlapping complex issues. Childhoods are not experienced within a vacuum, rather they are connected to a range of sociological issues such as class, ethnicity, gender and geographical location. Within society, children are holistically influenced by the type of early childhood setting they go to, their schools, their health care and the media. All of these issues impact on different children in different ways, and in these complex ways childhoods are understood in a holistic way. This knowledge of the complexity of childhood leads us to ask many questions about children. This is where the research tool can help us to begin to answer some of those questions. So, as an early childhood practitioner, you can begin to see why you must be engaged in research; there is so much more to learn about children and their varied childhoods!

JANE'S SMARTPHONE RESEARCH

In case study 1.1, think about how Jane's reflective observations of children coming into nursery in the morning gave rise to a whole series of interesting research questions. Notice how her thinking challenged her pre-conceived ideas and how the research would lead to improved knowledge and possibly changed practice.

— 🔍 —— CASE STUDY 1.1 ————————————————

YOUNG CHILDREN AND TECHNOLOGY

Jane had worked in a nursery school for several years and was knowledgeable about early childhood. However, over the past year she had been struck by how many children she saw in the nursery playground playing on their parent's smartphones and she reflected on how little she knew about what they were doing. When she asked some of the children about this, they showed Jane how they had opened the YouTube application and selected their favourite videos. Some of the children were able to show Jane how they could listen to different pieces of music and also showed her videos of themselves at home! Jane was amazed at how competent, confident and flexible these children were at navigating their way around these smartphones. She reflected on the differences between the children's competence with this smartphone technology outside of school and the limited ways in which those same children were using computers in the nursery. Jane wondered why there was this difference and how it might be overcome. She also realised how little she really knew about children's technology use other than from reading negative newspaper articles about young children playing too many games! From her informal observations at school and the anecdotes she had heard, she knew that there was a lot more going on!

Jane. wanted to read more about young children and technology. She was determined to 'dig deeper' and find out more about the educational value of smartphones, tablets and computers. She wanted to understand more about what children could do with technology and so she began to note down questions in her **research diary**. What, if anything, were the children learning whilst they were playing on these devices? What learning dispositions were being developed? To what extent was internet game playing, such as Club Penguin, going on at home? How did children interact with each other on the computer? What was the teacher's role in supporting children playing on the computer? What were the ethical issues around young children playing on the internet and how might these be understood?

THE PROFESSIONALISATION OF EARLY CHILDHOOD STUDIES

It is important to note that research is a powerful tool in developing early childhood professionalism (MacNaughton et al., 2010). So, whatever your motivations in coming to this book, whether to develop your critical skills in reading about research done by others or because you wish to carry out research for yourself, you will be helping with the ongoing professionalisation of early childhood studies.

You might want to know more about early childhood research for a variety of reasons: for example, it might be a compulsory project as part of your course assessment, or you might be a practitioner working with children in some capacity and wishing to carry out a small-scale study as part of that work with the intention of improving your practice in your institution. Such practitioner **action research** is increasingly important in developing and improving early childhood practice. This book will help you to ask research-style questions about your own current practice, the collection of evidence, its **analysis** and any possible conclusions that can be drawn. Early childhood practitioners are therefore increasingly recognised as key participants in the culture of childhood research.

By reading this book, you will inform yourself about what constitutes high-quality, valid research and this will make you a better 'consumer' of research and policy. By understanding the process of high-quality research based on ethical values and principles, you will be able to review and reflect on the research you have read more effectively and with greater confidence. By being aware of what constitutes high-quality ethical research, you will be able to critically evaluate research conducted by others. Such critical reflection on research carried out by others is central to the process of professionalism within early childhood studies.

By aspiring to be an 'evidence-based profession', early childhood practitioners move beyond merely responding to whatever the next government policy or initiative might be and adopt a more powerful and informed position. Much early childhood practice is currently led by government policy. By becoming an informed consumer of research and actually carrying out research yourself, you can generate your own knowledge and understanding. Such understanding is useful in the process of responding to policy initiatives. For example, by having read research evidence on emotional literacy in the early years and perhaps carrying out research on emotional literacy with children, you are in a better position to review government policies which address, or omit, emotional development in young children.

THE IMPORTANCE OF YOUR REFLECTIVE PRACTICE

Some early childhood practitioners incorrectly create a division in their own minds between an imagined 'academic high ground' and the 'swampy lowlands' (Schön, 1987). They feel that 'thinking about practice' (which is what reflective practice is) belongs to an 'academic high ground' which is not for them. These practitioners wrongly feel that they should just *do* practice and not *think about* practice. This is because they incorrectly believe that the 'practice' of doing early childhood research and 'thinking about it' are disconnected and separate. Such attitudes can act as a self-limiting barrier to one's potential. Practitioners who engage in reflective practice can produce real-world knowledge grounded within their work. By engaging in a process of reflective practice, practitioners can create real-world knowledge born from experience and critical reflection. Reflection involves thinking about a particular aspect of your work and how to improve it. This process of reflection is personal but it may also be done with your trusted critical friends and/or colleagues.

Reflective practice is about improving practice and generating the theories by which to understand that improvement. Such real-world knowledge produced by early childhood practitioners is as good as that within the 'established' academic community. In order to ensure that your real-world knowledge has **validity**, you must demonstrate that it involves critical reflection and a systematic enquiry. The key message is that early years professionals can and do produce original thinking. This is because although people may well have carried out research into your topic area before, nobody has ever done your particular piece of research in your particular setting before. Schön (1987) made a distinction between 'reflection in action' and 'reflection on action'. Reflection *in* action is about 'thinking on your feet', which is what early years practitioners do all the time, of course! Reflection *on* action is a more subtle and mature retrospective thinking or 'thinking after the event'. Early years professional reflective practice primarily involves thinking after the event about what happened and *why*. Your reflective practice research in your unique early years context may throw up original insights and thoughts about the topic area. By engaging in a systematic process of reflective practice research, your 'voice' will be heard in the field of early childhood.

With reflective practice, *you* take control of *your* situation: you are the script writer, the stage director and the main actor/actress. And yes, it is your play! You own the research and it is personal and meaningful to you. This is why reflective practice is so empowering. You become the insider researcher with the passion and enthusiasm to make insightful observations and improvements in your early years setting. You also become the expert doer and thinker. You can generate your theories as to what worked and why and perhaps learn from those changes that didn't work and the reasons for this. Here, your reflective practice and research generate *sustainable* change because the practitioner is central. The practitioner creates and implements their own ideas rather than the ideas of an outside expert.

WHAT DOES REFLECTIVE PRACTICE INVOLVE?

Reflective practice is concerned with you investigating and evaluating your early years work. Reflective practice is also concerned with you taking action to improve your personal, social and professional early years context. The main questions that early years reflective practitioners ask are based on the following:

- What am I doing?
- Why am I doing it this way?
- How can I improve on what I am doing?

These questions are at the heart of any early years reflective practice research project. From these practical projects, it is possible for early years practitioners to generate their own personal theories about what works in an early years setting and what doesn't work. Hence, reflective practice is concerned with *both* the practical aspects of doing your job better *and* generating knowledge about why you believe your practice has improved.

Table 1.1 contains some questions which highlight the differences between outsider-type questions (traditional research) and insider-type questions (action research).

Table 1.1 Outsider-type and insider-type questions

Traditional research questions	Reflective practice research questions
What is the relationship between children and the outdoor environment?	How can I improve the use of the outdoor area?
What is the connection between management style and increased motivation?	How can I improve my working relationships with my support staff?
Why do early years policy documents generally not include young children's thinking?	How can I listen more carefully to young children's ideas about what they think they should be learning?
What is the relationship between enhanced family involvement and children's learning?	How can I get families more involved in my early years setting?

In the questions in Table 1.1, you can see that you, the practitioner, are centrally involved in the research process: 'I' is used in all the reflective practice research questions because you, the practitioner, are central and you are asking questions about your professional work. You know your setting and yourself and, as a well-trained reflective practitioner, you also know the sorts of questions you need to ask to improve your practice. Reflective practice thus presents a fundamentally different approach from that of traditional research. Within reflective practice, you are much more powerfully positioned since you are in control of the process from start to finish.

STEPHEN'S REFLECTIVE RESEARCH QUESTIONS

In the following example, think about the ways in which Stephen's research was professionally reflective and empowering to him as a teacher.

Stephen was a Reception teacher and he had a deep belief in child-led learning through play. However, he was also concerned that over the past year senior colleagues had expected him to be more formally 'teaching' the children literacy, particularly phonics and maths.

Stephen felt that his play-based approach to learning was increasingly being challenged, questioned and undermined by the changes going on around him, and he wanted to know more about why these were happening. What policy amendments had enabled these changes and why? Stephen reflected on how he could own the research so that it empowered and further professionalised him. Hence, he asked the following questions: How do I make sense of and respond to increased school-readiness expectations in the early years? To what extent can I retain my **child-centred** values and philosophy? What can I do in the classroom to keep child-led learning central?

REFLECTIVE PRACTICE RESEARCH AS PROFESSIONAL DEVELOPMENT

Reflective practice is centrally concerned with your process of professional development, change and improvement. Practitioner research is an integral part of your critical professional development. As a professional, you constantly need to reflect on your work and the ways in which you enhance that work with young children. The underlying principles and values of reflective practice should be integral to everything you do in this regard.

As a professional, you will constantly need to reflect on your work. Increasingly, early years professionals need to be accountable so you will need to be able to justify what you are doing and why you are doing it. Your reflective practice project will help you understand an issue in much more depth. This understanding will then help you justify your professional actions. The following is a summary of some of the ways in which reflective practice research can help you develop your early years professionalism.

1.　A deeper understanding of your values and principles

Reflection involves thinking about a particular aspect of your work and how to improve it. This process of reflection is personal and may also be done with trusted critical friends or colleagues. Informed and insightful reflection is a central aspect of personal and professional development. This will lead to an enhanced understanding of your professional values and principles.

2.　Increased professionalism

By engaging in the process of reflective practice, you will develop your interests and motivation in your work, leading to further reflection and development. A positive cycle of personal and professional development can develop from your initial small-scale project.

3.　Enhanced working relationships with children, parents and colleagues

Reflective practice is very often a collaborative venture and can involve close working with colleagues, children, families and communities. Reflective practice can be a sociable experience carried out with trusted colleagues or critical friends.

4.   Developing your pedagogic skills and knowledge

Critical reflection can arise out of your desire to enhance your teaching skills and knowledge of how you can help children best develop emotionally, cognitively, physically and spiritually. Much practice with young children involves holistic learning. Reflective practice can be sensitive to the subtle and complex learning processes of young children.

5.   Increased theoretical knowledge and engagement

One of the great benefits of engaging in reflective practice is that it is your project and you may wish to develop not only your practical knowledge but also your theoretical knowledge of the issues. Your reading of other people's ideas about early years issues, together with your experience and insight, can generate your own knowledge and understanding about what works and why. In this way, reflective practice is empowering and can give meaning to practitioners' working lives. Early years workers engaged in reflective practice develop personal 'living theories' about themselves and their work. As you share these 'living theories', you will become increasingly confident in your own thinking and theories about your practice. This increased confidence and awareness of *why* you do *what* you do is part of your professionalisation process.

6.   Developed self-respect, power and self-esteem

Early years workers who engage in reflective practice projects feel more powerful. This is because action research is about you taking the lead responsibility for developing your personal and professional work. This can result in an increased sense of empowerment and enjoyment from your work. Action research can thus initiate positive cycles of personal and professional development. A worthwhile piece of action research that you personally believe in can empower and transform your working life. You will feel more powerful in your work as you come to reflect on and change it in various ways for the better.

7.   Increased respect for children

Some reflective practice projects involve listening to children's perceptions and understandings. Such projects can highlight what you already know, namely that young children are strong and have immense abilities and competencies if we allow them. It is we adults who need to listen to and see children better.

8.   Increased awareness of the wider contexts in which you work

Much of your work as an early years professional will be framed by various pieces of government legislation and policy guidance, such as the Early Years Foundation Stage (DfE, 2017). As you engage in your research project, your awareness will be raised of the wider policy contexts in which you, your work and your early years setting are situated. This increased awareness and knowledge may lead you to carry out further action research projects.

9. Increased confidence in your research skills

By carrying through a piece of reflective practice research, you will gain experience and knowledge of how to successfully plan and engage with a research project. This will develop your confidence in this key aspect of your professional development. You will be able to answer people who cite research and evidence with your own knowledge and understanding to justify what you are doing and why. This is a powerful and professional way to engage.

PRINCIPLES OF HIGH-QUALITY EARLY CHILDHOOD RESEARCH

Regardless of the topic of your research project, there are some basic principles which underpin all quality early childhood research. The underpinning values and principles of high-quality research can be summarised as follows (MacNaughton et al., 2010).

Your research should be:

- critical and political
- ethical
- respectful of children's participatory rights
- purposeful
- well designed
- transparent
- honest about your assumptions.

THE CRITICAL RESEARCH STANCE

Critical researchers would argue that at the heart of their research is a desire to *transform and change people*. For the purposes of a small-scale project, this transformation is often about the researcher themselves developing their understanding through enhanced knowledge and experience by actually doing the research. Ultimately, critical research is concerned with the transformation of people, their institutions and thus society itself.

Social justice is at the heart of any critical research. The principles underpinning critical research include fairness, justice, equality and respect. Chapter 2 describes some personal research stories in which all the researchers had issues of social justice they wished to write about. Such social justice issues included race equality, patriarchy and the violent oppression of women and children, unfair gender stereotypes and a desire to listen to children's perspectives in the schooling process.

The point is to keep a critical stance throughout the research process. In order to do this, researchers must continuously ask questions about their assumptions and underlying beliefs and be aware of the power issues within their topic. Issues of racism, sexism, classism, violence and the negation of children's rights do not occur in a political vacuum. Within critical research, the interactions and structures which allow such abuses of power and inequalities will need to be understood, discussed and challenged in your written work.

Critical research involves researchers being continuously open to alternative views and perspectives. Being critical can include being sceptical of the use of certain everyday terms. For example, critical researchers challenge the thinking that goes along with the label of special educational needs, preferring instead to work with the ideology of inclusion.

LEE'S RESEARCH: A CRITICAL PERSPECTIVE ON CHINESE AND ENGLISH EARLY CHILDHOOD DIFFERENCES

As you read the following example, think about how Lee's experiences in England have challenged her preconceived ideas about early childhood education. What assumptions has Lee had challenged by her experiences in England? How have her reflective observations and questions further professionalised her?

Lee was a student from China and when she came to England she was very interested to see how much free play, exploring and practical activities went on in English early years settings. Lee was also very intrigued to learn that children's emotional development was a central concern in many settings, rather than cognitive learning. In China, Lee was used to much more formalised learning taking place, for example she had formally taught 2-year-olds how to read and write through memorisation. The central prominence given to child-led activities, especially play, and the focus on learning characteristics and dispositions in England challenged her thinking about early childhood education. Lee wondered why there were such differences in attitude to learning between the two countries and what she could learn from these different approaches. Specifically, she wanted to know more about the advantages and disadvantages of each system.

ETHICS ARE CENTRAL

Ethical issues must be central to any piece of early childhood research. Ethical issues should continuously permeate all aspects of the research process, from the questions or hypotheses asked, to the choice of research techniques, and how the research is presented and fed back to the respondents. All research can potentially be both beneficial and, sometimes, inadvertently harmful. Your research should aim to make a positive contribution to the broader social good within early childhood. Think about the ways in which your project may be beneficial to the children, the setting and to you. You will also have to try to predict any possible ill effects your research topic and your questions might have. It is therefore crucial at the outset of any research to think through any possible ethical difficulties, problems and concerns that may arise as a result of your research. Think of these possible difficulties in relation to the children, the setting and you. If you are doing your research as part of a college course, ethical issues might determine whether it is possible to carry out the research or not. So, think through carefully any potential ethical difficulties now to avoid disappointment later on. Chapter 4 focuses on the ethical issues needing consideration in your research.

CHILDREN'S PARTICIPATORY RIGHTS

Children are important people within the research process and children have participatory rights in issues which affect them. So, within the research process, listening to children, consulting with them and respecting their views are becoming widespread in childhood research. Children actively wish to participate in the research process, for example in the planning of children's services. This process of actively engaging with children demands sensitivity from the researcher. The ethical considerations in participatory research with children are changing the ways in which research itself is understood.

PURPOSEFUL RESEARCH

Your research should have clear aims and be worthwhile. The research topic and what it sets out to do should matter to you and to others. If your research is worthwhile, it is likely to be interesting and enjoyable – essential if you are to complete your project! Purposeful, clear aims to the research are also vital in encouraging others to take part in your research.

YOUR RESEARCH SHOULD BE WELL DESIGNED

You should have carefully thought through your research approaches and techniques. Sufficient reading and knowledge will help to inform your research questions or predictive hypotheses, which should also be well thought through. The research should be well organised and achievable within a particular timescale.

YOUR RESEARCH SHOULD BE TRANSPARENT

Transparent research allows other people to follow your complete research trail. Hence, your research should be clear and honest. When other people read your research, they should clearly understand what you did and why you did it. Transparency involves letting people know why you took certain decisions within the research process, and is important for validity.

 ACTIVITY 1.1

Think about the assumptions that you hold regarding your research topic.

Write down any strongly held beliefs you have about your topic.

Why do you think you hold these beliefs about your topic?

ACTIVITY 1.2

Carefully read some newspapers/magazines for a week and collect examples of research that affects children and families and early childhood. Then answer these questions about the articles:

What do you think of this research?

Does it tell us anything significantly new?

Was it, in your opinion, worth researching and publishing?

Who might benefit from the research?

Does it fulfil the principles for high-quality research?

THE RESEARCH PROCESS WITHIN EARLY CHILDHOOD STUDIES

Research within early childhood can be approached in many different ways. Different overall approaches include perceiving research as a linear process or as a recursive spiral process.

In the linear model of early childhood research (see Figure 1.1), it is envisaged that there is a set of more or less fixed stages through which the research must pass in an orderly fashion.

The straightforward stages in Figure 1.1 provide a useful and necessary structure for your research. However, such a fixed model can prove to be rather limiting and constraining.

Stage one: *Choosing an early childhood topic*

Stage two: *Thinking about possible methods*

Stage three: *Reading about the early childhood topic*

Stage four: *Collecting the evidence*

Stage five: *Analysing the evidence*

Stage six: *Writing up*

Figure 1.1   The linear research model

The recursive research spiral is not a fixed process. It allows for the research to be more flexible and open to changes in direction. In this book you are encouraged to revisit any of the research stages in the light of your ongoing understanding, reading and evidence. In the spiral model, research becomes dynamic, fluid and open to change as you progress with your topic. For example, sometimes early childhood researchers can only select their topics after they have read some literature in the area they are interested in. Indeed, reading permeates all stages of the research process. At other times, a piece of evidence may emerge in the form of a child's drawing, or what

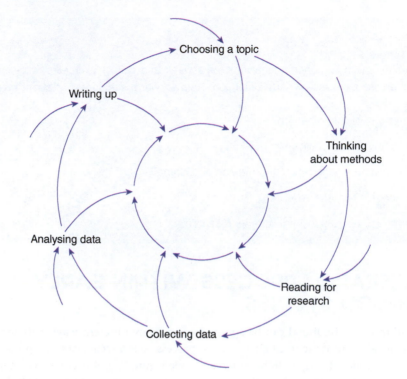

Figure 1.2 The research spiral

Source: Blaxter et al. (2010)

a child says, or a new initiative in your workforce which might lead you into reading and asking different and amended research questions. In these ways, the spiral research model is useful because it can be entered at almost any point.

EVERYDAY RESEARCH SKILLS

To get on your course or be employed within your work setting means that you are already experienced in many everyday research skills – whether you know it or not. However, you are probably unaware of how many research techniques you are already familiar with. Everyday research skills and techniques that you are experienced with will include:

- reading
- asking questions
- watching
- listening

- selecting and sorting information
- organising
- writing
- reflecting.

You will probably be very good at some of the above everyday research skills but might never have considered such an ability to be a research skill! For example, going on holiday with friends involves using many of the above everyday research skills. Finding out where to go involves selecting and reading appropriate magazines, websites and books. You may also ask friends and family for advice. You will have to reflect on the reading and your friends' advice to make a selection of where and when you go on holiday. You might decide to go to a travel agent. You will then have to ask a specific set of questions which might include destinations, costs, carriers, and travel arrangements for small children, elderly people, etc. You might have to think about appropriate clothes, language and money. You will thus accumulate a vast amount of material on destinations and travel which will need sorting through and organising. You will then have to make a selection based on your information. All of the above activities involve a huge amount of planning, organisation and effort. This book will make these implicit everyday research skills, that you already possess, explicit for you. All these natural skills and abilities that you already possess in order to book a holiday mean that you *can* successfully carry out a small research project. Table 1.2 clearly shows the connections between your everyday life skills and research skills.

Table 1.2 The connections between everyday life skills and their more formal research equivalent

Everyday life skills	Research equivalent
Reading	Reading for research; literature review; documentary analysis
Listening	Interviews
Watching	Observations
Choosing	Sampling and selection of respondents
Summarising situations, events, television shows, films, etc.	Managing your data
Organising events and situations within a given time frame	Managing your project
Writing	Writing up your project
Reflecting on life's events and situations	Researcher bias

ACTIVITY 1.3

Think of an 'everyday' situation that involves using research skills that you already possess, for example buying a new smartphone, choosing your child's childminder, organising a wedding, buying a car. List what you would have to do and the everyday research skills you would need to employ to successfully carry out the task.

SUMMARY

The principles and values underpinning high-quality early childhood research are crucial in producing critical social research that empowers practitioners, their institutions and the children in their care. This chapter has begun to demystify the process of research by making explicit the everyday research skills that you already possess. Early childhood studies is an area of rapid growth within society. As integrated and holistic children's services are developed throughout society, so early childhood practitioners' responsibilities are increased. Enhanced knowledge about children's complex and varied lives will help to meet these professional responsibilities. Your small-scale research project is an important part of this professionalisation process.

In this chapter, you will have:

- developed your confidence to 'have a go' at research
- understood the importance of your early childhood studies research project
- appreciated the significance of reflective practice in your research
- examined the principles underpinning high-quality early childhood research
- appreciated that research is a process and not a one-off right or wrong event.

RECOMMENDED READING

Department for Education (DfE) (2017) *Statutory Framework for the Early Years Foundation Stage: Setting the Standards for Learning, Development and Care for Children from Birth to Five.* Available at www.foundationyears.org.uk/files/2017/03/EYFS_STATUTORY_ FRAMEWORK_2017.pdf (accessed 8 June 2017).

MacNaughton, G., Rolfe, S. and Siraj-Blatchford, I. (eds) (2010) *Doing Early Childhood Research: International Perspectives on Theory and Practice*, 2nd edition. Buckingham: Open University Press. The second edition of this classic textbook is an excellent guide for both novice and experienced early childhood researchers. The first two chapters provide novice researchers with an in-depth and thorough discussion of the process of early childhood research and the principles of high-quality early childhood research.

Wilson, E. (2017) *School-based Research: A Guide for Education Students*, 3rd edition. London: Sage. This book is an extremely useful 'how-to' guide for early childhood researchers who are working in educationally based early years settings. Each chapter is clearly laid out and discusses the entire research process from start to finish.

WEB LINKS

www.learnhigher.ac.uk/research-skills – this is a fantastic, thorough and well researched website and the following sections are particularly useful; What is research?; Analyse this!!!; Collect this!!!

www2.le.ac.uk/offices/ld/resources/writing/writing-resources/planning-dissertation – this website carefully guides you through a reflective process of choosing a suitable early childhood research project.

www.postgrad.com/uk_research_planning – a website which contains succinct and appropriate advice on how to choose your research topic. For international students there is a particularly useful section on choosing to do research in your home country.

REFERENCES

Blaxter, L., Hughes, C. and Tight, M. (2010) *How to Research* 4e. Buckinghans: Open University Press.

Department for Education (DfE) (2017) *Statutory Framework for the Early Years Foundation Stage: Setting the Standards for Learning, Development and Care for Children from Birth to Five*. Available at www.foundationyears.org.uk/files/2017/03/EYFS_STATUTORY_ FRAMEWORK_2017.pdf (accessed 8 June 2017).

MacNaughton, G., Rolfe, S. and Siraj-Blatchford, I. (eds) (2010) *Doing Early Childhood Research: International Perspectives on Theory and Practice*, 2nd edition. Buckingham: Open University Press.

Schön, D. (1987) *Educating the Reflective Practitioner*. San Francisco, CA: Jossey-Bass.

For additional online resources, please visit **https://study.sagepub.com/roberts-holmes4e**

YOUR RESEARCH STORY, METHODOLOGY AND RESEARCH QUESTIONS

LEARNING OBJECTIVES

This chapter will help you to:

- reflect on the areas of early childhood in which you have a deep personal and professional interest
- understand that your methodology is central to your research
- start to formulate your research questions.

REFLECTING ON YOUR PERSONAL STORY

The aim of this chapter is to help you think of an appropriate early years research topic. This topic needs to be appropriate for you both personally *and* professionally. You should try to choose an early childhood research issue which is deeply stimulating to you personally – the heart aspect – and, at the same time, is of practical professional use for your future career – the head aspect. You will need to think both passionately with your heart and strategically with your head. Choosing the right topic at the start is important because it is difficult to change this halfway through.

This is your research, so the motivations for doing it need to be selfish. You need to own and take responsibility for your research project to complete it successfully. To begin with, you need to think of a topic in which you ideally have a deep personal and passionate interest. This interest may come from your work experience or may come from family and personally lived experience. So, within this chapter where work experience is referred to, this might equally be your lived personal experiences with family and friends. Such professional and personal enthusiasm will lead to the high levels of motivation needed to sustain your interest throughout the research process.

People choose their research topics for a variety of interrelated personal and professional reasons. Some research topics stem from our personal lives. For example, you may have experienced a significant incident in your life which might lead you to ask further questions about that incident. Sometimes such critical incidents may have occurred with your family, or perhaps at work, and you then wish to find out more about the particular issue. Research is sometimes about our own storied lives and making sense of ourselves. Hence, when choosing a topic to research it is good to look deep within ourselves to find one in which we have a personal interest. This may involve reflecting on our own lives and perhaps on critical incidents that have occurred within those lives. Such personal reflection and introspection are not always easy and indeed may prove to be emotionally problematic. You should not be afraid of this, since such reflection might well lead you to locate a personally significant and important research topic.

METHODOLOGY

Methodology refers to the principles and values, philosophies and ideologies, that underpin your research (Clough and Nutbrown, 2012). The methodology that you hold structures how you perceive and understand your research topic and the knowledge that you construct. You may espouse a variety of values and principles and thus your research may have several methodologies. For example, you could have a child-centred methodology, a feminist methodology and an anti-racist methodology that together will underpin your research. These deeply held principles and values, which drive your desire to carry out a piece of research, will form the basis of your research methodology. Reflecting on your research story will help you become more aware of your methodology. If the reason you are carrying out a piece of research is to take children's voices seriously, then your research will have a **child-centred** methodology. This child-centred methodology will then inform the questions you ask, the literature you read, the methods you use, and how you analyse your **data** (Clough and Nutbrown, 2012). As a result, your methodology, that is, your principles and the values concerning your topic, will inform the entire research process.

SOME RESEARCH STORIES

When reading the following personal research stories, ask yourself the following questions:

- How have the researcher's personal and professional issues been combined?
- What drove and motivated the researcher to carry out their research?
- What were the researcher's underpinning methodologies?

KATY'S PERSONAL RESEARCH STORY

I live in London and my boyfriend is Jamaican and a lot of our friends are African and West Indian. I'm really interested in the different ways in which black and white children learn about their identities. How do children learn their racial identity? This is my personal interest. My friends' kids are so aware of race even though they're little, you know, 3- and 4-year-olds. They're really interested in the colour of my skin and their skin. They'll say my skin is white or peachy and that they have brown skin. I'm really interested in these children's knowledge. Nurseries and schools are really really important in helping children to learn their racial identity so that's why I'm doing my project! There was also a really good lecture on race here and that made me think even more about how important multi-cultural education is. I'll probably work in London as a social worker on a SureStart project in a mixed area, and it's important that I understand everything I can about these issues and be knowledgeable about the latest research. So this research project will be really good for my career.

KATY'S METHODOLOGY

Katy's research project was closely connected to her social situation and hence was meaningful and important to her. Katy's research was motivated by her concern with issues of social justice for ethnic minority children in early years settings. Her values and principles came from a deeply held conviction about the injustice of racism, especially when directed towards children. Thus, the methodologies underpinning her research were child-centred and anti-racist.

LUCY'S PERSONAL RESEARCH STORY

Lucy's research concerned women and children and domestic violence. The **ethics** of this difficult and sensitive issue meant that Lucy's research was limited to asking professionals about domestic violence. Clearly, for a novice researcher, first-hand research with the victims of domestic violence was not appropriate:

> When I was little I had a violent father. I have grown up hating violence. I am now so interested in this topic that I will be reading about it in the summer after I have handed my research study in. I am emotionally strong enough to carry out this research since I have gone through counselling and it was years ago. I have a family of my own now and have discussed it with my children. I feel very strongly about the issue. I feel it's something I really want to further investigate. I want to know what laws and policies and practices are in place to prevent domestic violence from occurring. What do schools, if anything, tell children about domestic violence? I want to help in some way because I am a survivor and am now in a position to help other victims. So I want to have more knowledge about the problem. The research is not just about therapy for me, although inevitably there is a bit of that too, but rather so I can improve my knowledge and get a job in the area. I'm quite determined to do this. My research has shown me that the children's viewpoints of domestic violence are often overlooked in all this. Also that professionals working with children are often unsure about domestic violence.

LUCY'S METHODOLOGY

Through the research, Lucy wished to develop her self-understanding and raise awareness about domestic violence amongst professionals working with children. The human rights of women and children to be free from violence and fear drove her research. Lucy's methodology was thus feminist and child-centred. These deeply held values informed her reading, methods and the analysis of her research.

MARK'S PERSONAL RESEARCH STORY

> In my research I wanted to find out about how other men experience the early childhood setting. I'm disabled and doing this course has proved to me and to others that I've been able to overcome my health difficulties. I've proved to people that my health is not an issue and now I find that I have got to prove that my gender is not an issue. It's funny really 'cos I knew that my health issues would be a struggle but I never thought that my gender would be a struggle.

> This research project is good preparation for my own working life as a man in the early years. What prejudices does society hold about men in the early years and how do other men deal with such prejudices? The research project has made me feel more knowledgeable and wised up about being a

man in the early years. Hopefully it will now be a bit easier to cope with. I've found out about other men's personal opinions and achievements despite the prejudices and this has really grabbed me. I've just got drawn into some articles and books which are so interesting that I just want to find out more.

MARK'S METHODOLOGY

Mark's personal research story centred around his identity as a disabled man who wants to work with young children. The political context of his research was concerned with gender and disability equality in the early years. His underpinning methodology was gender awareness within the early years and the inclusion of people with physical impairments. The research provided Mark with insights into the stereotypes that exist about men in the early years. With the knowledge gained from his research, Mark had become more knowledgeable and confident about being a man working in the early years.

SARAH'S RESEARCH STORY

I worked in a play scheme and I thought that the friendships that the children formed were really fascinating. These 2- and 3-year-old children came in, not knowing each other and yet quickly some of them got on with each other very well. These young children made such strong friendships in such a short space of time. They looked forward to seeing each other every day and if someone was away they would ask after them! I found it amazing to watch. I can clearly remember an incident in which I was trying to comfort Anna, a 2-year-old girl, who had just started nursery. Maisy, another 2-year-old girl who hadn't been at the nursery very long herself, came up to us and gave Anna a big hug, saying 'wants mummy'. I found the ability to empathise at this early age and the desire to help each other quite fascinating. I remember a lecturer quoting from Piaget saying that toddlers were egocentric and didn't empathise. Well, this wasn't my experience! It made me want to read more about young children and friendships. I mean, how do they learn to get along so quickly like this? It was so interesting to see.

I also worked in a school and saw some children who had poor self-esteem and few friends. I was interested in that too. So my general topic of interest focused on friendship, which seems to be so important for children and their emotional well-being.

This research has given me an insight into the emotional development of children's friendships and how sociable children really are. I would like to be a family counsellor, but in the short term I want to work for a charity that helps children and their families.

SARAH'S METHODOLOGY

Sarah's work experience showed her that young children could empathise with other young children's emotional states at a very young age. She had found this 'fascinating', particularly because it contradicted what she had heard in a lecture about toddlers being egocentric and unable to empathise. Sarah had a deeply held conviction about the social competencies and social abilities of young children. This child-centred research methodology then led her to use participatory and child-centred research methods which listened to and took seriously children's perspectives and viewpoints (Lancaster and Broadbent, 2010).

GAIL'S PERSONAL RESEARCH STORY

My son is in a Reception class at the moment so that's a strong motivation to look at this topic. I'm hoping that in the future learning will be an enjoyable thing for my son because at the moment he absolutely hates school.

I am a really strong believer in play. I have worked for many years in a nursery and have seen how children benefit from play. I think my son hates school because there is not enough emphasis on play. I just don't believe in Reception class that they should be made to hold pencils and taught to write on worksheets. I have an issue with worksheets and they use them every day at my son's school. I just don't agree with this. They should be learning about themselves as learners. All children should be doing stuff to build their self-esteem and social skills and get all the basic skills before they move on. Play is children's natural way of doing this.

The philosophy behind the Foundation Stage Curriculum Guidance seems to be brilliant. It is play based, but the philosophy is only as good as the people who implement it. With my research I was trying to make the practitioners aware of their practice. It's really important that teachers reflect on their practice. So my research was about encouraging this reflection and for the teachers to see what they were doing. I wanted them to know that I knew what they were supposed to be doing with my son. I really wanted them not to do the worksheets with my son.

Soon after, I read an article on children's perceptions of school and what they thought school was for and what work and play were. This triggered my ideas off and made me realise that I could do research into this area. Before I read this article I wasn't sure if I could do this research or not.

GAIL'S METHODOLOGY

Children's rights, including a child's right to play, was the social justice issue at the heart of Gail's study. Gail was centrally concerned with the happiness of her son as he started school in Reception class. From her experience and reading, she believed that young children like her son should be learning crucially important social and emotional skills through play rather than be pushed into formal learning at too early an age. Gail's passionately held belief in children's right to play led her research to be underpinned by a child-centred methodology.

YOUR REFLECTIVE DIARY

It is important to carry out such personal reflection on your own and in your own time. Your personal motivations are part of generating the methodology, validity and authenticity of the research project. To begin with, give yourself 20 minutes to scribble down any autobiographical ideas that come into your head. Over the course of a few days and weeks, revisit the areas of personal interest in your life and see how these issues connect together. This can be done with a handwritten diary or on your computer. Such notes can be kept and will then begin to make up your personal research diary. Such a personal and confidential research diary will help you in the process of formulating a meaningful research topic and research questions.

Add into your diary the discussions you have had with family and friends and work colleagues about the children in your centre, and possibly your own children. Much high-quality early childhood research will begin with a researcher's own children. You may have observed something in the children at your centre or school which really interests you. Perhaps you and your work colleagues and friends and family have been discussing a particular early childhood issue which has fired your interest and you would like to know more about it. Try to look out for the connections between these observations and your autobiography.

The mass media of television, newspapers, magazines, radio and the internet is constantly reporting on and creating childhood crises and concerns. In your research diary, you should try to keep note of any such articles or programmes in which you have been particularly interested. If you are a student, you may have heard something in a lecture or seminar which you would like to follow up on.

With all the above inputs in your research diary, you should aim to keep yourself and your deep personal motivations centre stage. Try to see how the other inputs from work colleagues, family and friends, lectures, the media and books build on *your* personal interests. You come first, not the other way around!

ACTIVITY 2.1

The following pointers and questions will help you in writing up your reflective research diary:

1. What am I really interested in doing and why?
2. Where am I coming from and what are my reasons for choosing this research project?
3. What do I want to change by doing my research?
4. What is the political context of the research?
5. What is the methodology driving my research?

Some of what you write might be confidential, in which case, do not share it with anybody else. Due to the sensitive ethical nature of early childhood, there are some topics which it is not ethically possible to research. You might find it useful to share some edited versions of your story with a friend, and possibly your tutor. In addition, you may want to edit and develop further some of what you have written for inclusion in the written project itself.

HIGH LEVELS OF MOTIVATION

It is vital that your research project is personally meaningful to you because you will need high levels of motivation to complete it successfully. It is this enthusiasm and the desire to know that keeps Gail up at night and gets her out of bed early on a wet Monday morning! Such motivation will encourage you to work hard, as Gail records:

> If I was doing something I really wasn't interested in I wouldn't have the heart to sit there and read a book about it – 'cos I'm so interested I want to read about it. If you're really interested in it you don't mind sitting there at 10.00 at night reading a book – you want to know. I send everybody out, including the dog, so I can read! It is such an interesting issue. You really have to be passionate and fascinated and want to make a difference.

Gail wanted her research project to make a difference for her son and her own understanding of the issues of play in early childhood education. As was the case with Gail, some researchers are seeking enhanced clarity around issues that they have long had a personal interest in. Many wish to gain insights into the area that they are researching in order to develop themselves in some way. Such personal change can lead to enhanced self-confidence and self-esteem flowing from enhanced insight. Enhanced confidence in the area of their interest might lead to job applications in that particular area. Lucy, who looked at the issue of domestic violence, initially wanted to be a teacher:

> ... but that's not for me now. This research has given me the confidence to apply for jobs in the area of domestic violence. I now want to work as a domestic violence officer coordinating an educational initiative. When I go for interview I know what to say and which questions to ask. This project will really help me when I start work.

Lucy's research project, which had deep personal meaning for her, had developed her insight and confidence in the area so much that she was applying for jobs in the area of domestic violence and preventative educational projects.

PROFESSIONAL MOTIVATIONS

Be selfish with your choice of research topic. Choose one that will be of benefit to your career. You are investing a tremendous amount of time and resources in your research project so make that research count and work for you. If you know the area of early childhood in which you wish to pursue your career, try to arrange a meeting with someone in that profession: for example, a nurse, a teacher, a SureStart project worker, a nursery manager. Ask them which areas of early childhood need researching from their professional point of view. Lucy's research focused on a range of early childhood professionals' understandings of domestic violence. This knowledge would have helped her secure a job as a domestic violence education officer. If you hope to become an early years teacher, choose an educational topic and appropriate Key Stage setting. If you wish to become a speech and language therapist, choose to study an issue within this topic in the appropriate setting. If you wish to work in some aspect of the SureStart projects, then choose to study an area of this major government project in its context.

If the professionals' ideas fit with your personal interests, then wonderful. If your personal ideas are different from their professional needs, then perhaps you can work out a compromise. If you are a further/higher education student, then you must discuss your research topic with your tutor and supervisor. Tutors can often build on ideas for a research topic and possibly suggest career pathways.

ACTIVITY 2.2

As you think strategically about your career, answer the following questions:

What areas of early childhood would you like to work in when you complete your course?

How can your research project further your career?

What work opportunities might arise as a consequence of your research?

Have you seen your college/university tutor?

Have you chatted with a professional in the area?

Have you talked your research ideas through with your family and friends?

FOCUSING ON YOUR AREA OF INTEREST

One of the most important ways of finding the specific area you wish to investigate is to read relevant articles and books, check websites, view television documentaries, reflect on your work experiences, and talk through your ideas with your friends, family and tutor. All of these information sources are essential in order for you to begin to formulate opinions and views on key issues within your topic area. From your reading and discussions, various ideas will emerge and you will be able to see just how complex your topic area is. New possibilities and interests within the topic area will keep opening up. At this early stage in the research process, such new ideas and avenues within your wider topic area are to be welcomed. As a result of your reading and discussions, your specific focus may shift and change. Further reflection within your research diary may lead you to change your focus again. Such creative shifts in the focus of your research are normal and healthy and a creative part of the research process.

Once you have decided on your general topic of interest, you should try to focus on a specific area. At some point within the process of exploring your general topic area, you will have to make a decision about what it is you *specifically* intend to research. A good research study will have a particular and specific focus. When starting your research, it is easy to explore many different and interesting routes towards your research ideas. This is valid and healthy but your work can then rapidly lose focus. Many interrelated areas connect with childhood studies, such as education, health, sociology and anthropology. Each area has its own literature and interest in childhood. It is important, therefore, that your personal study area is as focused as possible. Five stages can be identified in this focusing process:

1. Identify the general area in which you are interested.
2. Read, read and read in the general area – find out what others have said and done in your area.
3. Reflect on your work experiences and talk your ideas through with your family, friends and tutors.
4. Carry out a **pilot study**.
5. Try to identify the specific issues within this area in which you are interested.

In case study 2.1, identify the general area that Sam is considering researching:

- What are the four specific issues that Sam could research?
- Is Sam's research sufficiently focused?
- Do you think this is a problem at this early stage?
- What should Sam do in order to focus her research?

— 🔍 —— **CASE STUDY 2.1** ————————————————

Sam worked part-time in a Reception classroom as a teaching assistant at a local primary school. She was also enrolled to do a childhood studies degree and had to carry out a small-scale research project. Sam had three brothers and had always been interested in issues of gender at home and then at work. Whilst at work, Sam wondered why so many boys played with the Lego whilst the girls chose to play in the home corner. This interest in gender issues was confirmed at college by a stimulating lecture on gender and childhood. Sam then began to read in the area of gender and became fascinated by the 'nature-nurture' debate. Why did boys and girls act so differently at such an early age? Back at work, Sam became more interested in the gendered aspects of her work. Why were all the classroom assistants and teachers female except for the male head teacher? She spoke to her friends at other schools and this confirmed that there was only one man working in the early years in her town. She wondered why this might be.

At playtimes, Sam observed how boys and girls would often choose to play in separate gender groups. She found some articles on the internet about children and friendship groups and became very interested in gender and friendship and what the connection might be.

In the classroom, Sam had noticed how some of the girls seemed to be much more interested in reading books and writing stories than did some of the boys. She knew that the girls' interest in reading and writing in Reception was connected with girls doing better at tests in Year 2 and Year 6 of primary school. She had a hunch that this was to do with the lack of positive male role models in the boys' lives and wanted to find out more about their home lives. Sam was interested in finding out about the school policies and practices that existed to encourage boys to become more interested in literacy.

In case study 2.1, Sam was going through the normal process of talking and reading as she attempted to specifically identify the focus for her research topic. She had decided that her general interest lay in the area of gender. Through her work experiences, chatting with friends, and library and internet literature searching she had developed many related gender interests:

- gender and friendship
- gender and literacy

- gender and inclusion issues throughout school
- teachers' gender and career issues.

Each of the above issues is so big that they could be the worthwhile study of four separate investigations in their own right. Sam would have to decide on which of the above gender issues she would pursue further.

After further reading and reflection at work, and discussions with her tutor, Sam decided to concentrate her project on gender and friendship groups. She made this choice because the other issues were too big for the six-month time frame allowed for her project. She had a good relationship with the children and wanted her study to encompass children's gender and their friendship groups.

ACTIVITY 2.3

Look at the general research area that you are interested in. Now try to make this general research area more focused and specific to one particular issue.

What is it exactly that you wish to find out more about?

Complete these sentences:

In my research study I wish to find out more about …

I want to look at this specific issue because …

Writing your research questions will help you focus your interest on a specific area.

THE OVERALL RESEARCH QUESTIONS AND FIELD QUESTIONS

There are two main types of questions in research. The overall research questions structure and frame the research project and, to a certain extent, are answered by the whole project. This chapter is concerned with these large overarching general questions of the study which define and clarify the limits of your study. The field questions are the actual specific detailed questions that the researcher asks people in **interviews** and on **questionnaires**. Chapters 6, 7, 8 and 9 look at the more detailed questions which you would actually ask people in an early childhood setting. These field questions are then used later in your study to collect evidence for your project to answer the overall research questions.

The large overall research questions are important because they:

- define the limits and context of your study
- clarify the purposes of the study
- help to concentrate and focus your thinking, reading and writing on the specific area

- help to clarify the methods – that is, sort out what you actually need to do
- keep your research heading in the right direction for the duration of the study.

GETTING YOUR RESEARCH QUESTIONS RIGHT: BREADTH AND DEPTH

It is a difficult but vital task for a researcher to make their research questions 'just right' (Clough and Nutbrown, 2012). Getting the balance of making your research questions sufficiently broad to make your work interesting, and at the same time focused enough so that you can actually answer the questions in your short time frame, is quite a skill.

A good research study has specific and doable research questions. Your research questions will keep bringing you back to exactly what it is you are looking at in your work. The wonderful thing about good research questions is that they will help that work to have both breadth and depth. On the one hand, your research questions need to be sufficiently broad to engage with the wider political and social context of your work. Your research study needs these wider connections to make your study relevant, significant and interesting. On the other hand, the questions must be specific and detailed so as to ensure a depth and clarity of purpose in your work. Such specific questions will help to ensure that your work does not ramble. Your questions also need to be doable and realistic for you to answer within your limited timescale. When your tutor finally marks your work, he/she will be looking to see whether or not your study has answered your overall research questions. Writing specific and doable research questions is a process. In the light of your ongoing reading and discussions, these will shift and change.

ACTIVITY 2.4

Do your research questions allow your work to be sufficiently broad to engage with the wider issues?

Are your research questions specific and focused enough to avoid your work being rambling and disconnected?

Look back at Sam's case study (2.1). What follows demonstrates the questions that are too big or too small, and those that may be considered just right for Sam's purposes.

SAM'S RESEARCH TOPIC ON GENDER AND LITERACY

The following are three research questions which are too big:

1. Why do the boys not read very much and why do the girls read a lot?
2. Why do girls do so much better at tests at school?
3. What sorts of things do boys like doing at school?

These questions are too big because they do not define the limits of the study and as such are unfocused. The context for the research has not been established. Which boys and girls, and where-abouts are they located? The questions also carry assumptions concerning *all* boys and *all* girls, and such issues have not yet been established. The third question does not relate to the first two.

Now, here are three questions which are too small:

1. Is Jack a good reader because his father is a teacher and reads with him at home every night?
2. What impact on Jack's reading was there after reading a football magazine with him?
3. Is the fact that Jack is left-handed significant for his literacy development?

These questions are clearly too small to be of sustained interest over a period of time. They focus on one boy and make assumptions about his literacy development. The project would have more validity if it encompassed a wider range of children and viewpoints. The final question focuses on one literacy event and ignores the girls.

Here are three questions which are specific and doable:

1. How do all the various stakeholders within the children's centre understand the term 'literacy'?
2. Within the children's centre, what are the various contexts for literacy events?
3. What similar and different literacy events do boys and girls participate in?

The first question opens up the concept of literacy. This question allows all the members of the school – the children, the teachers and the parents – to define how they understand literacy. It is an inclusive question and begins to point towards methods for actually collecting the evidence for the study. The second question allows the study to explore those literacy events that occur within the children's centre. This question encourages the researcher to observe and critically watch what goes on in an early years classroom. It is a sufficiently broad question to allow that researcher to make connections from many observed relationships and activities towards an inclusive definition of literacy. The third question focuses on the gender issue. Only after having established what literacy is and why, and in what contexts it occurs, can we focus on gender and literacy. The question pointedly states that there will be similar and different literacy activities with the boys and girls. This question will prevent a researcher from making generalisations about all boys and all girls.

ACTIVITY 2.5

Now try to write three or four specific questions for your research topic. Remember that writing research questions is an ongoing process and it will take you several attempts until you are completely confident of them.

For each question that you write:

- reflect on whether it is too big or too small until you feel that it is 'just right'
- go through all of these and ask yourself 'What do I need to do to find an answer to this question?' In this way you will begin to identify the actual tasks that could be done to answer each question – for example, library research, questionnaires, interviews, observations, diaries, drawings and photographs.

DOING A PILOT STUDY

A pilot study often involves gathering evidence and information from people before you carry out the larger study. A pilot study can help check that your research topic and research questions and planning are proceeding along the right lines (Figure 2.1). A pilot study is critical at the beginning of your study because it will alert you to whether or not your research questions,

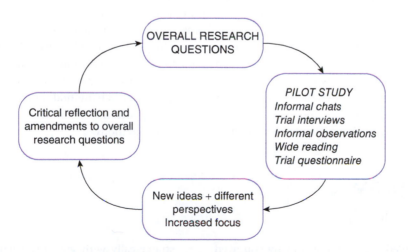

Figure 2.1 The relationship between the overall research questions and the pilot study

approaches and proposed research methods are specific, ethical and actually doable. In light of the findings from your pilot study, your research questions and plan might well need refining and rephrasing with some changes. Such changes to your plan must be seen as a positive step because a pilot study is concerned with reflecting on and revisiting your work to date.

LUCY'S PILOT STUDY

For her pilot study, Lucy had informal chats with two teacher friends and a domestic violence officer about her research project. She also trialled her interview questions. She needed to do this to clarify in her mind what the field questions would be for her **survey** questionnaires. Lucy was interested to note that in each of three open-ended discussions remarkably similar issues arose. A lack of adequate training and knowledge as to how to respond to children who were experiencing domestic violence was an unexpected recurrent theme. These and other issues formed the basis of the themes asked about in her questionnaires which she then sent out. In addition, she then trialled the questionnaires themselves.

SARAH'S PILOT STUDY

Sarah's pilot study included a series of observations in the classroom in which she was to carry out her research on friendships. As Sarah watched and talked through her plans with the classroom, she realised that she would have to be much more focused in her topic. She observed that friendships in the classroom were based on a whole range of issues, including socio-economic class, race, gender, children's self-esteem, age, networks outside school, the teacher's planning and responses to children, physical disability and ability. Although each of these issues contributed to children's friendship in some way, Sarah needed to focus on just one issue. She chose the issue 'friendship and gender' for her focus. However, Sarah was aware that the issues mentioned above might be just as important as gender and acknowledged this as a limitation within her study.

Such pilot observations also served the purpose of helping the children to build up a relationship with Sarah and learn to trust her. The pilot study reinforced what she had read about children perceiving her as a teacher and how this would impinge on their spontaneity in discussions with her. This realisation led her to adopt drawings as a research method, since the children seemed to draw freely and spontaneously when given the opportunity, hence the importance of the pilot study in alerting her to more appropriate research methods.

SUMMARY

This chapter has:

- provided the reasons as to why you need to think passionately with your heart and strategically with your head when planning the area you wish to research

- discussed the central importance of keeping a reflective personal diary
- discussed the critical role of research questions in helping you to focus on a specific issue

- demonstrated the ways to write focused overall research questions.

RECOMMENDED READING

Clough, P. and Nutbrown, C. (2012) *A Student's Guide to Methodology*, 3rd edition. London: Sage. Chapters 1 and 2 present sound arguments for your work being personal and making connections with wider political issues. These two chapters also provide compelling case studies for reflecting on your personal learning journey by doing research.

Hallet, E. (2016) *Early Years Practice*. London: Sage. This user-friendly text has an excellent first chapter, 'The reflective early years professional', to help promote your reflective thinking about your research topic.

Visit https://study.sagepub.com/roberts-holmes4e for a video of the author's top tips from this chapter.

WEBSITE LINK

socscidiss.bham.ac.uk/methodologies.html – this is an extensive website that provides an all-encompassing overview of the entire research process and can be dipped in and out of for a deeper understanding. There are useful links and references to further reading.

REFERENCES

Clough, P. and Nutbrown, C. (2012) *A Student's Guide to Methodology*, 3rd edition. London: Sage.

Lancaster, Y. and Broadbent, V. (2010) *Listening to Young Children*, 2nd edition. Maidenhead: Coram Family and Open University Press.

For additional online resources, please visit **https://study.sagepub.com/roberts-holmes4e**

3

WRITING YOUR LITERATURE REVIEW

LEARNING OBJECTIVES

This chapter will help you to:

- understand why a literature review is necessary
- organise your literature review
- recognise the kinds of literature you should be reading and writing about
- discover where that literature is located.

WHY YOU SHOULD DO A LITERATURE REVIEW

At first, you may wonder why wlriting a literature review is necessary at all and it may seem daunting and overwhelming to you! However, don't panic because the purpose of a literature review is simply to let your readers know what is happening in your particular early childhood research area, so it is really not too daunting. After reading this chapter, you should be clear on why a good literature review is an essential part of a research project and how you can write this review. A key part of a good research project is becoming familiar with the main ideas and arguments in your research topic area. A good literature review is essential in demonstrating that you understand where your research fits in with all the other research carried out in your topic area. The literature review forms its own chapter within your research project. The same literature is then built on, expanded and developed to analyse your data in research findings and discussion chapters. So the literature review is a key part of your research project.

READING WIDELY

The first part of doing a literature review is to read widely in your chosen topic area. Whatever it is that you have chosen to study in the early years, there will be lots already written about it! People hardly ever have completely new ideas, so no matter how random and obscure yours may seem, there will be published material on that topic. So, the first thing to do is to engage in some wide reading around your topic area and it really doesn't matter at the early stages what that literature is! This initial reading will help you see that the area you are thinking about contains many arguments, ideas and points of view.

— 🔍 —— CASE STUDY 3.1 ———————————————

Elizabeth was interested in assessment in the early years. She approached this topic by reading anything that interested her in the area, including what she found on the web and in 'quality' newspapers and professional magazines as well as book chapters

(Continued)

and articles. She combined this wide reading with her own professional knowledge and experience.

This initial reading combined with her experiences convinced her that there was too much formal assessment focusing on maths and literacy. Elizabeth agreed with the points of view that suggested that formative child-led 'learning stories' were more useful than a separate literacy and maths summative assessment.

CASE STUDY 3.2

Jenny was interested in researching the benefits of outdoor play. At first, she thought that not a lot had been written about this topic, but as soon as she had begun to search for outdoor play on the internet she discovered that a huge amount had been written about outdoor play. In the early stages of her reading, Jenny knew that it was fine to read anything and everything about outdoor play, and the ideas she found on the internet really fired her enthusiasm and interest. She came across a wide range of material which looked at the following areas: Forest School and Scandanavian approaches; outdoor play equipment and safety concerns; 'messy' play; different cultural and historical attitudes to outdoor play; weather and clothing; colleagues' and parents' views; outdoor play with animals; creative and imaginative outdoor play and resources; and barriers to outdoor play and how to overcome them. Jenny's initial wide internet search had led her to a lot of interesting ideas, but she realised that over time she would have to sharpen her focus to examine just one area of outdoor play. However, her initial internet search confirmed that the exciting area of outdoor play was the right choice for her!

DEVELOPING YOUR OWN POINT OF VIEW

One of the most important reasons for carrying out and writing a literature review is to help you clarify and focus your thinking about your research topic. On the one hand, you need to develop your own point of view on your topic and, on the other hand, you need to stay open to unfamiliar ideas and not be biased against them. Developing your line of argument and, at the same time, being open to new ideas and possibilities that challenge your existing thinking will lead to critical thinking, reading and writing. To help you develop your ideas about the topic and to further focus your thinking, it makes sense to find out what other early childhood researchers have to say about your topic area, and this will then also help you to see that your topic fits into a range of existing ideas and arguments. Discovering how your reading fits within a wider 'body of knowledge' will help you develop your own thinking on which of the arguments and points of view you agree with. This process will in turn develop your all-important point of view or line of argument about a topic. Therefore, as you read, you will begin to recognise what you think and feel about your topic and this will help to strengthen your particular point of view and therefore your line of argument. As you read, reflect on your own professional experiences and perhaps your lecture notes and see how these connect with the arguments in the literature, as in Figure 3.1.

Figure 3.1 Developing your point of view

You can see that being well read, combined with your own personal and professional experiences (and perhaps lecture notes), is key to completing a successful research report. The literature review is vital because it enables you to be knowledgeable about your area, and so able to develop a set of coherent and logical arguments about your topic area.

CASE STUDY 3.3

ANDREW'S DEVELOPING POINT OF VIEW

Andrew wanted to look at the role of rough and tumble (R&T) play in the early years. As he started reading, he soon discovered that there were many arguments for and against this type of play. Andrew realised that he believed that this form of play was a positive aspect and felt that it should be encouraged in early years classrooms. Hence, Andrew's reading and reflecting led him to understand his own point of view which in turn helped him to weave a set of arguments supporting R&T play. He also recognised that it was important to discuss opposing arguments that said R&T play was problematic. He knew that it was necessary to discuss and weigh up the evidence from both perspectives, whilst at the same time maintaining a line of argument in favour of rough and tumble play. In the following short extract presenting both the arguments and counter arguments, Andrew maintained his point of view that R&T play was important, demonstrating good writing:

(Continued)

Flanders et al. (2010), in a longitudinal study involving 19 boys, 15 girls and their fathers, argued that the quality of father/child R&T play is a defining factor in the development of a child's ability to successfully regulate aggressive impulses and interpret others' emotions. Smith (2010) also emphasised the importance of R&T play for young children's social development, particularly a child's ability to read emotional expressions and their ability to understand the signals given by play partners (Smith, 2010).

Panksepp (2008) suggested that R&T is one of the most valuable forms of play in that, whilst engaged in it, children experience three, of the eight, positive emotional states that are genetically ingrained in the brain: seeking, care and play. It is now well documented that the absence of play has profound effects, from inflexible and patterned behaviour to violence and other anti-social behaviour (Brown and Webb, 2005; Marks-Tarlow, 2012). It has even been proposed that there may be a link between the increased prevalence of attention-deficit hyperactivity disorders (ADHD) in young children and the decreased opportunities for children to engage in the types of physical play that so crucially promote the maturation of higher brain capabilities (Panksepp and Scott, 2012).

However, tensions between parental concern over their children getting hurt and the growing body of research that suggests that children actively seek challenging play that involves some risk, are still felt in schools (Sandseter, 2013). Rough and tumble play is particularly recognised as carrying a degree of risk of harm to the participants and as such becomes a potential site for concern (Smith, 2010; Sandseter, 2013). Factors such as more stringent child protection procedures and a higher profile given to the safeguarding of children within the Ofsted framework for assessing schools (Ofsted, 2013) have contributed to what Sandseter (2013: 13) terms as 'a strong risk aversion' concerning children's play environments. This has led to a narrow focus by parents and practitioners on physical injury (Bundy et al., 2009) and a blinding of them to the dangers that result from restricting children from physically active play. These include child fragility, obesity and restricted emotional, intellectual and social development, and an increase in the likelihood of suffering from ADHD (Marano, 2008).

Importantly, your literature review places, contextualises and situates your research ideas within the existing written and published material. This shows that your thinking and ideas are not unique but instead fit in with and connect to the material that has already been published on your topic. In this way, a literature review helps you see how your study is connected and related to the existing ideas, arguments and debates within the literature that you have found. Your early wide reading will show you how your ideas connect with what has already been written about in the area. You might also begin to see how your research can build on and develop this!

WHAT YOU SHOULD READ AND INCLUDE IN YOUR LITERATURE REVIEW

After your initial internet searches on Google and Google Scholar, you will see that there is a vast amount of information, articles and government policy and initiatives on every early childhood topic. At first, as you develop your ideas, thinking and arguments, it will be a good idea to keep your reading as wide as possible. The 'literature' that you find on Google can generally be divided into two types: 'grey literature' and 'peer reviewed' literature. These are summarised in Table 3.1.

Table 3.1 Grey literature and peer-reviewed literature

Grey literature	Peer-reviewed literature
• Collaborative early years online chatrooms, e.g. EYFS chatroom	• Library books and e-books
• Personal wikis and blogs	• Journals and articles
• TV/radio/internet, e.g. BBC education	• Government policies
• Local education authority (LEA) websites	
• Professional magazines, e.g. *Nursery World, Early Years Educator*	
• Videos/DVDs	

GREY LITERATURE

Grey literature (such as an early years blog or wiki or magazine article) may be very interesting and perhaps make strong arguments that you find attractive. You might well agree with these arguments and ideas and they could help you focus your own thinking. Such literature has a valuable place in informing you about the latest developments within early childhood and may offer useful critiques of government policy. However, blogs and wikis are rarely referenced and tend to simply present a writer's personally held points of view based on their particular lived experiences. Similarly, some magazine and newspaper articles will present a biased point of view without any supporting references. Such sources of information, whilst interesting, are not considered trustworthy by the academic community since they are usually not based on established research techniques and are not generally included within a literature review.

PEER-REVIEWED LITERATURE

Academic literature and grey literature do not have equal status. Your tutor will not be impressed with grey literature references so use these very sparingly, if at all! However, as noted, grey literature can be useful since it is immediately available on the web in response perhaps to a government initiative, whereas academic literature takes longer to be published. Peer-reviewed literature is more reputable, trustworthy and valid because it is usually based on high quality and valid research which makes the articles convincing and reliable. Peer reviewing means that the article (or book) gets sent to expert early childhood academics who will carefully read the material and decide whether or not the article is of a sufficient quality to be published. The whole process is anonymised so that the expert academic does not actually know who the writer of the article is! This ensures fairness and transparency, so it is not just friends and colleagues who get published but the best from around the world (which might include you).

ACTIVITY 3.1

AN EXAMPLE OF USING RESEARCH ARTICLES TO EXAMINE AN ISSUE

In the following short extract, you will see how a Chinese student found scholarly research articles which argued that Chinese early years teachers do not support play for learning. Note the number of research articles she has used.

Vong's (2005) research in three Shanghai nurseries found that Chinese teachers' cultural beliefs did not value the role of play in learning. The 12 teachers in the study felt awkward encouraging children's learning through play since it was counter to their cultural beliefs. The research noted that the teachers were more at home with the traditional didactic approaches to teaching and were reluctant to replace it with playful pedagogy (Vong, 2005). In Li et al.'s (2012) research, 19 early years classes in three cities in China were observed and the findings suggested that teachers were not willing to follow the Western play ideas due to their firmly established cultural understanding that play and learning were distinctly different. Sha (1998) examined parents' and teachers' perspectives on play and reported the huge influence of Chinese culture on the implementation of play. It was identified that play was only used as breaks between early childhood teaching sessions (Sha, 1998), which was consistent with the Chinese cultural interpretation of play as divorced from learning. Indeed, in Wu and Rao's (2011) large-scale survey, Hong Kong teachers reported that they considered play as aimless and hindering children's early learning.

USING YOUR COLLEGE/UNIVERSITY ONLINE DATABASES

Using Google and Google Scholar, it is possible to see the articles in your topic area that are available. Such a basic search will usually provide you with just the article name and abstract and you will then need to log onto your college/university system to access the full e-versions of these articles through Google. Once you have done so, you will have to carry out full searches for your area of interest within any of the early childhood journals listed below.

SOME PEER-REVIEWED EARLY CHILDHOOD RESEARCH JOURNALS

Journal of Early Childhood Literacy

Journal of Early Childhood Research

International Journal of Early Years Education

Play

Early Childhood Development and Care

European Journal of Early Childhood Research

Early Years: An International Journal

Contemporary Issues in the Early Years

Other well-known journals which carry early childhood articles:

British Educational Research Journal

Journal of Education Policy

British Journal of Educational Sociology

So, for example, you might want to carry out a literature search on early years and the benefits of outdoor play, and hence you could begin by searching through back copies of the *Journal of Early Childhood Research*. First, find the web page for the journal and then enter your search words into the search box at the top right of the page. Make sure that the 'within current journal' is clicked, otherwise it will search through all the Sage journals. (See Figure 3.2 for an example.)

Once you have found an interesting article, you must first read the abstract. If after reading the abstract and perhaps scanning the article's sub-headings the article does indeed look interesting, then you can open the full article in the pdf format and save it for a later and more thorough reading. It is fine to print out such key articles and then mark them up and underline the key points and quotes you wish to use. Sometimes you will come across an article or a book or chapter that you will find incredibly powerful, convincing and significant in your topic area. You might also discover that you deeply agree with its arguments and ideas and wish to develop those arguments. Such articles and books are very useful because you can then follow up their references and sources, since these will show where their initial ideas and arguments came from. Finding such 'gems' can greatly strengthen your arguments as you build on such key articles. Very often, a good academic writer will have written several books and articles, and by searching for their name through Google and Google Scholar you can identify their other pieces of writing. This can be a fantastic way of doing your literature

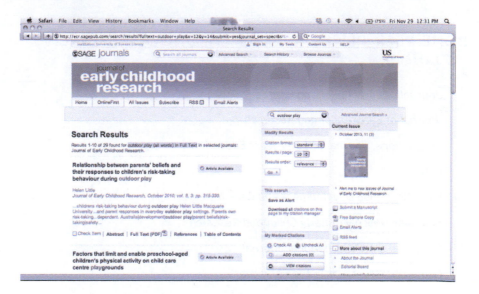

Figure 3.2   Journal search

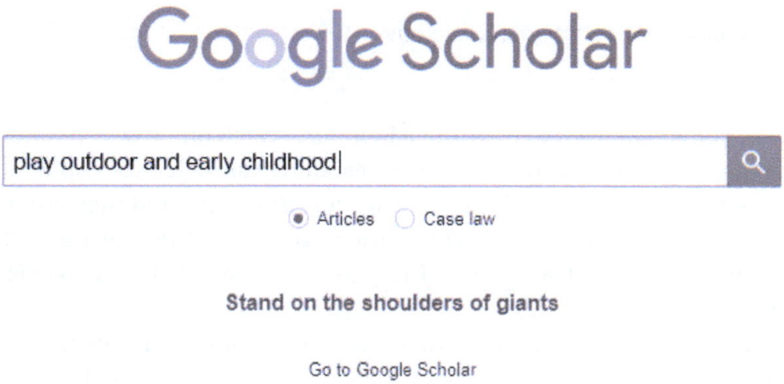

Google Scholar

play outdoor and early childhood

● Articles   ○ Case law

Stand on the shoulders of giants

Go to Google Scholar

Figure 3.3   Google Scholar

Source: Google and the Google logo are registered trademarks of Google Inc., used with permission

review. However, although it is always nice to follow a particular writer's point of view, do remember to include any counter arguments as well so that by doing so you provide a balanced and well-rounded argument!

USING GOOGLE SCHOLAR

Google Scholar is one of the most commonly used academic online search engines because it is user friendly and you can easily filter your searches for exactly what you want. You can filter your search to find recently published articles, books and conference papers. For example, Jenny used Google Scholar to track down academic articles on early years outdoor play by simply entering the words 'play', 'outdoor' and 'early childhood' into the search box. By using Google Scholar, Jenny located 25 high-quality and trustworthy peer-reviewed academic research articles and books, all of which were of potential interest. Some of these articles were fully available online through Google Scholar and she saved other references by signing into her Google Scholar account. Then when she logged into her academic library she was able to gain full access to the articles. Google Scholar also highlights books that contain the key words in the search engine and again you can then search for these in your online academic library.

HOW TO READ A REALLY USEFUL ARTICLE

Ideally, you will want to build up and collect about a dozen or so really useful articles that are appropriate for your research topic. Store these articles digitally and possibly print these out to go through thoroughly, depending on your preferred reading style. On the next read-through, you will need to spend perhaps three quarters of an hour or so on each article and note down your thoughts in a simple table.

ACTIVITY 3.2

Before you look at the example below, read through the following article by Jackie Marsh (available on the Sage website for this book, at **https://study.sagepub.com/roberts-holmes4e**):

> Marsh, J. (2010) 'Young children's play in online virtual worlds', *Journal of Early Childhood Research*, 8(1): 23-39.

> As you read this, highlight the sections of the piece that show the main argument and research methods used.

> Now take a look at Table 3.2 in the case study. Did you identify the same key points as Jane? Is there anything in this article that might be useful for your own research?

— 🔍 ——— CASE STUDY 3.4 ————————————————

Jane had noticed that some of her nursery children played on their parent's smartphone as they came into the nursery each morning. She had asked the children what they were doing and some were watching YouTube and others playing games. She was interested in the positive benefits of digital technology for young children, so using Google Scholar she entered the key words 'young children digital play'. This brought up many interesting articles, and after having read the abstracts Jane decided to initially focus her attention on an article by Jackie Marsh (2010). Jane made the grid in Table 3.2 to help her read and take notes on the article; you can adapt this grid to your own style and needs.

Table 3.2   Jane's grid for reading research articles

Questions to ask	Jane's notes on Jackie Marsh's article
What do I like about the article?	Child-centred investigation of children's online games. Really exciting, positive and interesting article looking at children's online play with games such as *Club Penguin*. A refreshing and innovative look at young children playing with digital games like *Club Penguin*.
What is the article's main argument?	Online games can be safe, fun, and encourage talk and sociability with friends and family.
Which research methods are used?	38 5-7-year-olds did online questionnaires, with teacher support, and 10 did focus group interviews.
Can I use any of the research methods?	Yes, focus group discussions about digital play are a good idea. But I don't think the online questionnaires are child friendly. How about observations of children playing online games together and recording the dialogue of children playing on the computer? What about drawings?
Is there sufficient support and evidence for the claims that the article makes?	Yes, it's an incredibly detailed case study with a large number of school children who did an online questionnaire. Analysis is thorough and rigorous throughout.
What's the main 'takeaway' argument(s) from the article?	Online gaming and young children often seen as problematic and negative but Marsh problematises this by saying it can be positive and highly social. Children make connections with their friends between 'virtual' play and 'real' play.

Jane's grid contained a question about the research methods that the article used. This means that sometimes you can get some really good ideas about the innovative and creative research methods that other researchers have used. So another advantage to reading research articles is that they can inform you of a wide range of possible research methods, some of which you might wish to adopt for your project. You might also want to underline and copy some really good quotes from the article, but do be sure to keep a note of the relevant pages.

If you undertake the actions listed above for your dozen or so really useful articles, you will build up a great set of notes and ideas for your literature review. By approaching each of your favourite articles in this systematic way, you will have created a really good knowledge base and set of notes for your research area. Add to this the chapters in books that you have written up and you will be well on your way to a successful literature review.

DRAWING A MIND MAP

By now you will have thoroughly read about a dozen articles and chapters and made notes reflecting a balanced set of arguments and counter arguments about your topic area. At this point, you are ready to begin putting these notes into a coherent form. The first thing to do is to structure and organise your thoughts by drawing a 'mind map' or 'spidergram' showing the links and connections between the literature's key ideas. Figure 3.4 will give you a visual representation of your ideas and you can begin to see how these link together in graphic form. This shows Jane's mind map for her literature review on digital technology and play.

This plan is crucial since academic writing is about persuasion and the structure of your argument is critically important for convincing readers of your argument. You can add to and amend your visual organisational map as you wish and you can also number your ideas so that you can follow the structure of your arguments.

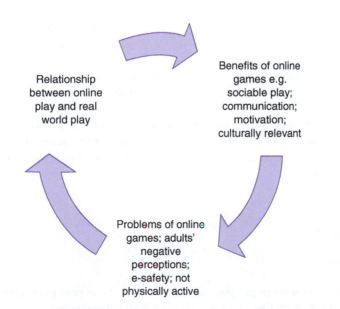

Relationship between online play and real world play

Benefits of online games e.g. sociable play; communication; motivation; culturally relevant

Problems of online games; adults' negative perceptions; e-safety; not physically active

Figure 3.4 Jane's mind map for her literature review on digital technology and play

SYNTHESISING THE IDEAS

Synthesising the ideas simply means that you bring together all the arguments for and against a particular topic and make sense of them as a whole. Doing so will integrate all the various ideas you have read about in one document in a coherent and logical order. The key point here is that the literature review is not just a summary of everything you have read but also a purposeful argument weaving all the arguments and counter arguments together. The wonderful thing about writing is that as you actually do it, you can see this idea synthesis developing in front of you! Sometimes your ideas will change and develop, so if that happens remember to go back to your 'mind map'.

WRITE, EDIT, RE-EDIT AND RE-RE-EDIT!

Unfortunately, there are no short cuts to the writing process and you will need lots of self-discipline, focus and time! Finding a supportive and encouraging context in which to write is essential. It may be that you prefer to work at night when it is quiet, or you might choose to write in a library, or you perhaps have a lovely office to work in! It doesn't matter where or when you write, but it must work for you and be a space where you can focus, concentrate and dedicate your time to writing. Good writing is about concentrating for long periods of time, so do find somewhere to hide! You will also need to dedicate plenty of time to editing and re-editing your writing, and as you do so your arguments will become clearer and clearer.

So, good writing requires the following:

- writing a balanced argument with ideas and opposing ideas
- synthesising all of your ideas together in one piece of writing
- a quiet space to concentrate in
- a developed plan with sub-headings based on the arguments
- using the literature to back up your arguments
- drafting, writing, editing, re-editing and re-re-editing.

Congratulate yourself and celebrate when you have written a section and sent it to your supervisor to read. Don't be put off if there are several corrections and comments. Just work through these systematically and go to see your supervisor face to face, if necessary, to discuss anything you don't understand.

SUMMARY

This chapter has:

- discussed various ways to get you started with your literature review
- examined how to search for appropriate literature
- looked at how to organise and write your literature review.

RECOMMENDED READING

The University of Edinburgh has a helpful website on mind mapping. You can find it at: www.ed.ac.uk/schools-departments/information-services/help-consultancy/help-services/online-help-guidance/students/it-help/guides/mind-mapping

Wilson, E. (2017) *School-based Research: A Guide for Education Students*, 3rd edition. London: Sage. This book offers great clarity with detailed and grounded advice about how to write your literature review with case study examples.

Wyse, D. and Cowan, K. (2017) *The Good Writing Guide for Education Students*, 4th edition. London: Sage. This is a fantastic text that will take you through the nitty-gritty of actually writing your literature review. The book is full of really useful top tips for writing an excellent literature review.

Visit https://study.sagepub.com/roberts-holmes4e for a video of the author's top tips from this chapter.

WEBSITE LINK

www.rlf.org.uk/resources/what-is-a-literature-review – this is a really useful in-depth website that carefully guides the reader through extended and thorough advice on how to write an excellent literature review for early childhood research.

REFERENCES

Marsh, J. (2010) 'Young children's play in online virtual worlds', *Journal of Early Childhood Research*, (1): 23–39.

For additional online resources, please visit **https://study.sagepub.com/roberts-holmes4e**

4

ETHICAL ISSUES IN EARLY CHILDHOOD RESEARCH

LEGISLATION AND THE PARTICIPATORY RIGHTS OF CHILDREN

Seeing children as valuable participants in the research process has come about as a result of legislation and changing sociological perspectives. Today's research ethical codes and practices have their roots in the Nuremberg Code (1949) which was established in response to the Nazis' research atrocities in concentration camps. The Nuremberg Code stipulates the following:

- the absolute *necessity* for the voluntary consent of research subjects
- the need to ensure that the research is for the good of society
- any unnecessary physical and mental suffering is to be avoided

- an assessment of any potential risks to the research subjects
- the necessity of allowing research subjects to withdraw from the research at any stage of the process.

The United Nations *Convention on the Rights of the Child* (UNCRC) (UN, 1989) provides a framework for addressing rights relating to children's need for care, protection and adequate provision, *and* their rights as regards participation. It aims to protect and promote children's rights and welfare through a set of principles made up of 54 legally binding articles. **Article 12** of the Convention is the most significant for research purposes because it declares that children have the right to hold an opinion about issues concerning them: 'State parties shall assure to the child who is capable of forming his or her own views the right to express those views freely in all matters affecting the child' (UN, 1989: Article 12), hence children have the right to be included in research which affects them. Although lacking legal status in the UK, Article 12 was ratified by the UK government in 1991, and clearly represents a major cultural shift towards the recognition of children as full participating members of society in the same way that adults are. It requires that adults respect the rights of children. With regard to research, Article 12 means that 'children have the right to be consulted and taken account of, to have access to information, to freedom of speech and opinion and to challenge decisions made on their behalf' (Morrow and Richards, 1996: 91).

At the same time as encouraging their participation, the UNCRC recognises that children are vulnerable, by placing the child's right to participate alongside their right for protection.

The UNCRC demands a cultural shift away from working *for* children to working *with* children, since the power balance between adults and children has shifted in favour of children. Such an objective has been given impetus by the Children's Commissioner who, by listening to, talking to and carrying out research with children, 'speaks up for children and young people so that policymakers and the people who have an impact on their lives take their views and interests into account when making decisions about them' (Landsdown 2011).

The Children and Families Act 2014 represents a further major legislative impetus in listening to and acting on children's voices and opinions in research. It encourages those who work and research with young children to listen to the voices of children and ensure that they participate in the research process.

Soon after the UNCRC (UN, 1989) was introduced, the British government passed the Children Act 1989. Like the UNCRC, the Children Act established that children should have the right to be heard about matters affecting their welfare. Both the UNCRC and the Children Act have had considerable impact on any research concerned with children because they encourage children's participation in the research process.

SOCIOLOGY AND THE PARTICIPATORY RIGHTS OF CHILDREN

Children have, until relatively recently, been seen through the lens of deficit and social pathology. Children's social competencies and their abilities were negated within a pathological model of childhood which centred on their low chronological age. Hence, children's needs and wants were interpreted by the adults around them, who spoke for children. Young children were seen as lacking in social competency and insight. Indeed, they were constructed not as human *beings* but rather as human *becomings*. Children could only gain social competency once they were fully developed adults. Thus, within this negative model of childhood – that is, what children *cannot* do – they were perceived as having little of significance to offer the research process.

Increasingly, children are viewed as socially competent and as 'experts in their own lives' (Langsted, 1994). It is seen as imperative that researchers include children's understandings and experiences in studies which may affect them. Indeed, researchers working with children are actively encouraged to *listen* to children and to take their views seriously. Malaguzzi (1996: 10) suggests that children are 'rich in potential, strong, powerful, competent and, most of all, connected to adults and other children'.

Ethics is centrally concerned with the attitudes of the researcher. If a researcher's attitude is one of respect for children's abilities, then that researcher is likely to use a variety of methods to listen to children's voices:

> If we, adults, think of children as powerful, they act powerful. If we treat them as powerful, they rise to our expectations. Indeed they can blow the tops of our heads off in terms of what they can do, if we choose to stand aside and let them, and see them in their true colours. (Drummond, 2002: 3)

Question: In what ways does your research project allow children to surprise and astound you with their abilities and social competency?

CHILDREN'S PARTICIPATION AND PROTECTION

The complex relationship in research with children between their *participation*, on the one hand, and their *protection* from risk, on the other hand, *must* be given due consideration by the researcher. The impact of participation on children may have all sorts of institutional and personal benefits for those children. However, it is essential that a researcher is reflective throughout to ensure that the impact *is* beneficial and not causing a child unnecessary stress and anxiety.

All research carries with it the *potential* for risk amongst the **research participants**, both children and adults, and for the researcher themselves. Such risk is often *inadvertent* because, clearly, the researcher does not set out to emotionally upset people but, despite the best of intentions, such emotional upset may occur. However well intended, research questions can and do touch on sensitive issues for children and adults. Children can be made to feel quite vulnerable by questions which intrude on their personal relationships with their families and friends. Researchers with the best of intentions might also, by accident, frighten and worry children by stirring up issues and events that are difficult for them. Questions might make the child think there is a problem with them and/or their family. Children are particularly vulnerable to difficult questions when a researcher is unfamiliar with them and their lives.

Whilst encouraging children's participation in the research process, it does need to be noted that some research projects carry with them the potential for negative impacts on children. One such possible negative impact is the invasion of children's privacy by enquiring adults. It is an irony that the more imaginative and sensitive researchers become to listening to children, the greater the possibility of further intruding into their private worlds. Thus, participatory research might be seen by children as yet another form of observation and surveillance of their lives by controlling adults.

A further concern is that researchers who rush to engage with the participation agenda might use disempowering research techniques such as one-to-one interviews and questionnaires. Asking children to engage with such inappropriate methods might lead to confirmation of the myth that young children cannot participate in research. A further potential negative impact of participatory research is that it might be perceived by the children as tokenistic. Tokenistic participatory research projects have little or no action following consultations with children. The problem with such research is that children might soon become disillusioned with the nature of participation if they perceive that what they say is subsequently ignored in practice.

It is the responsibility of ethical researchers to ensure that any such risk is *minimised*. One possible way of doing this is through the process of carrying out an impact assessment. The objective of an impact assessment on children is to encourage researchers to be critically reflective about any aspects of their research which might lead to their upsetting any of the participants, and especially children.

A REFLECTIVE IMPACT ASSESSMENT OF RESEARCH ON CHILDREN

Colleges and universities have ethical guidelines and ethical committees which are based on professional codes and guidelines. A useful list of web links to such guidelines can be found at the end of this chapter. If your research project is being carried out for a qualification through a college, then your research plans must be scrutinised according to your college's ethical guidelines. Your ethical discussion will show the readers of your report that you were aware of your ethical responsibilities regarding your respondents' participation and protection.

The following questions can be used to help organise your thinking and writing concerning ethical issues in your research:

- What potentially sensitive issues are raised by your research questions?
- What are the various ways in which your research questions might be inadvertently taken the wrong way?
- How might your questions cause the research respondent to worry in any way after you have finished?
- Could your research questions inadvertently have any negative impact on relationships within the early childhood institution?
- Could your research questions inadvertently have any negative impact on family relationships?
- In what ways does your research make the institution and its members vulnerable to potential criticism?
- What advantages to the respondents and their early childhood institution might there be from your research?

If you are concerned about any of the above questions, perhaps you should reconsider your research questions. If you are feeling that your questions might make children vulnerable in any way, then it might be preferable not to work with children as respondents this time. Perhaps because of your relative research inexperience, you might consider carrying out a particular piece of research at a later stage. Some inexperienced first-time researchers who are wary about upsetting children will include children's voices *by proxy* in their research. That is, they will not carry out the research with the children themselves and will instead refer to literature in which such research with children has already been carried out. If you choose to incorporate the voices of children by proxy, then you can state in your report why you are doing so. Lucy's research on domestic violence included the voices of children by proxy and this is discussed later in the chapter.

YOUR EMOTIONAL VULNERABILITY

As discussed in Chapter 2, research can be introspective and may unconsciously focus on unresolved personal issues. Generally, for the inexperienced researcher the best advice is to stick to research topics which are relatively emotionally safe. Any potential risks can be minimised early on at the planning stage of the research. There may be the odd occasion where both you and your supervisor feel you can proceed with an emotionally difficult subject. Lucy's research, for example, was concerned with the issue of domestic violence.

When Lucy went to her research supervisor with the suggestion that she investigate the issue of domestic violence, her supervisor was understandably initially concerned. As a mature woman with her own family, Lucy explained that over the years she had come to terms with the domestic violence she had experienced as a child and had forgiven her now dead parents. Nevertheless, Lucy stated that she was aware of the potential emotional risks involved for her in the research and reflected on her emotional state throughout the research. Her research supervisor made the decision that Lucy was sufficiently reflective and mature to proceed with the research.

— 🔍 —— CASE STUDY 4.1 ——————————————————————

ETHICALLY REFLECTIVE RESEARCH WITH CHILDREN

Initially, Katy, a white woman, had wanted to talk with her friends' children about their racial identities. Her friends' children were black British and mixed heritage and she knew some of the children quite well. However, on critical reflection of her research questions, Katy felt that the research could potentially and inadvertently upset some of the children. She had read that fostering and developing a positive, healthy and strong racial identity amongst children could be an emotionally complex and sensitive issue (Siraj-Blatchford and Clarke, 2000). On reflection, she realised that she did not know the families as well as she thought she did and was concerned that she might inadvertently intrude on complex family situations and dynamics. She also considered how the research questions might leave the children anxious and questioning about their identities when previously they might never have considered them to be an issue. She also became aware that as a white woman she did not have the same racial experience and insight of a black woman or man. A black person might be more sensitive in fostering and encouraging a positive and confident self-image amongst the children. After critically reflecting on these issues, Katy realised that her research could have the opposite effect of her intentions; that is, the research might inadvertently undermine the children and make them more vulnerable and anxious concerning their developing sense of self and racial identity. She realised that perhaps a more experienced researcher might be more appropriate in this instance.

Katy decided to examine the ways in which two nurseries promoted the children's ethnic identities. Rather than focusing on the children, with all its associated potential for risk, the research was to now focus on the institutions and what they were doing to encourage children's racial identities. Taking the spotlight away from the children and focusing it on the nurseries' staff, curriculum and resources *minimised* the risk to the children. As a result of their adult power and professionalism, the practitioners in the nurseries were less vulnerable than the children to any inadvertent harm.

However, Katy noted in her research report that, because 'race' is a politically important topic, nurseries might feel threatened by her research. Nurseries are now inspected by the Office for Standards in Education (Ofsted) to see that they are in accordance with the Race Relations Act 2001, in which nurseries, along with other educational institutions,

(Continued)

have a duty to actively *promote* the development of children's racial and cultural identities. Katy appreciated that the nurseries, by allowing her in to do research in this area, were potentially making the institution and therefore themselves vulnerable to any criticism. Katy therefore assured the nurseries of the utmost importance of confidentiality and that the institutions would not be recognisable in her report. She made it clear to the managers and teachers that her research was primarily concerned with her learning about how the nursery successfully promoted children's racial and cultural identities. By unequivocally stating that the research report was for her and her college tutor, Katy sought to minimise the nurseries' apprehension and she successfully gained access to the two institutions to carry out her research.

Lucy was aware that, with such a sensitive subject, direct research with the victims of domestic violence was clearly not an option. Hence, she did not carry out any direct research with the victims of domestic violence. Her study was limited to professionals, including nursery practitioners, teachers, family liaison officers, social workers and domestic violence officers. Such professionals have the necessary distance, **objectivity** and professional training to discuss such sensitive issues.

Lucy wanted to include children's perspectives on domestic violence in her research report and these she gained *by proxy* from the literature and the internet. This method of including children's voices by proxy is useful for inexperienced researchers when investigating sensitive subjects. If you have concerns about the ethical implications of carrying out research with children, this method of including children's voices by proxy from the literature is a safe alternative.

INFORMED CONSENT AND ASSENT

Informed consent refers to research participants *voluntarily agreeing* to participate in a research project based on complete disclosure of all relevant information and the recipient's understanding of this. Gaining the participants' informed consent to carry out the research is part of building trust in the relationship between yourself and the research participants. Trust requires that as a researcher you are honest and reliable and communicate all aspects of the research process to all the participants, as they have a right to know about the complete research process. Trust will develop over time as you honestly share your aims, methods and findings with them. Young children's informed consent is legally known as **assent** because they are deemed too young to provide informed consent. Careful thought needs to be given to translating this into practice when the research participant is a young child. For example, to what extent can a very young child understand the information that they have been given?

As a researcher, you must ask yourself whether the children have been given all the information about the research that they need to make a decision as to whether to participate or not. Such a verbal explanation is best done with small groups of children or with individual children. Specifically, have you told the children in words that they can understand:

- what the research is about?
- what you hope to accomplish?
- about their role?
- about the benefits and consequences of participating in the research?
- what you will do with their views and any visuals that you take?

- how their views will be documented?
- how confidentiality will be upheld?
- about the choice they have to consent or not to participate?
- about the right they have to withdraw from the project at any time?

You must give the children time to discuss any questions they may have concerning the above.

INFORMED CONSENT, CONFIDENTIALITY AND CHILD PROTECTION

It is important that, *before* children and other research participants give their informed consent and actually participate in the research, they understand there is a *limit* to the anonymity and confidentiality that can be given regarding what they tell the researcher due to child protection issues. This is because where a child tells the researcher that they are at risk of harm, or the researcher suspects that this might be the situation, the researcher has a *duty* to take steps to protect the child. Here, it becomes the researcher's *duty* to inform a child that you will be telling a responsible adult, usually the key worker or the teacher and your college supervisor, what they have told you. Thus, there is a limit to the confidence which you as the researcher can keep. Respondents, including children and young people, should be told at the outset, and as necessary during the research, that confidentiality cannot be guaranteed if 'difficult' information is disclosed. If, on discussion with the child, you decide it is necessary to inform others – hopefully with the consent of the child – you must then ensure that the child has immediate support and is kept fully informed. You should also immediately discuss the situation with your college supervisor if any child protection issues arise.

ACTIVITY 4.1

Read case study 4.2 and answer these questions:

How did Jane fulfil her duties as a responsible and ethical researcher?

In what ways did Jane follow the ethical guidelines?

——— 🔍 ——— **CASE STUDY 4.2** ————————————————

JANE'S RESEARCH ON UNDERSTANDINGS OF CHILDHOOD

'One child started to tell me about some abuse that was happening at home. I stopped the child immediately and said that if she wanted to continue to talk about it that I would need to talk to someone else about it as well. She was happy with this, and the information was passed on.'

Jane told the class teacher and her college supervisor and subsequently found out the girl was under close monitoring from the school and social services as a potential victim of domestic violence.

'On another occasion I was very concerned about a boy's constant referral to death and dying – I did not have the skills to help him, and so again, with his permission I passed the information on to his class teacher. However, my ethical commitment did not end there, for it was important to ensure that something had been done.'

Jane was sensitive and realised that there may well be an unresolved emotional issue for this boy. With the boy's agreement, she told his class teacher and her college supervisor. The teacher informed Jane that the child had recently suffered the particularly painful bereavement of his father. The school contacted the boy's mother and asked if he might like further counselling. Subsequently, the mother agreed and the boy received further bereavement counselling. Jane's compassionate sensitivity was of paramount importance in highlighting this child's emotional needs.

INFORMED CONSENT LEAFLET FOR CHILDREN

When working with children, in addition to telling them about the research, it is also good practice to produce a child-friendly leaflet outlining the research and what is expected of those children who choose to participate. Older children will be able to read the leaflet on their own but younger children will need help, so it is a good idea to read it through with all children whose parents/ guardians have given permission for their child to participate in the research. Even if the children are not yet able to read the leaflet on their own, it is a good idea to write an information leaflet for children and then read it with them. Writing and talking through such a leaflet with children and adults will help you think clearly about the nature and purpose of your work. This will improve the standard of your research and make it easier to explain to children and adults. Writing and reading through the leaflet reproduced in case study 4.3 with the children and adults involved in Jane's research was a key part of meeting her ethical obligations for the research.

As a corollary to the above inclusive and participatory research method, it is useful to remind ourselves about *disrespectful* ethical methods for research with children. Alderson (2008) gives an overview of such methods. These include:

- not respecting their privacy and confidentiality rights
- making covert observations, such as through one-way mirrors, or secretly doing case studies, video and audio tapes
- discussing the children openly without altering their names or hiding their identity
- assuming that the children are not yet able to speak for themselves
- asking adults (parents, teachers) for their views about a child's beliefs and behaviours but not also asking the child
- asking only negative and standard questions about children instead of also asking about each child's strengths, achievements and unique individuality
- using questionnaires with adult-centred questions such as 'What is your housing status?' that might make children look foolish
- labelling children without asking about their reasons, which might make sense of their actions and views
- testing them in labs, without seeing that being in a strange place can unsettle and distract them and thereby lower their competencies
- routinely using upsetting methods, such as the tolerance of strangers test to see how babies react if their mother suddenly leaves them with a stranger
- using deception, such as telling a child not to touch something without giving any reason, and then secretly watching them to see how long the child obeys
- talking down to children
- publishing results that reinforce negative stereotypes about children and young people.

⎯ 🔍 ⎯ CASE STUDY 4.3 ⎯⎯⎯⎯⎯⎯⎯⎯⎯⎯

JANE'S RESEARCH ON PERCEPTIONS OF CHILDHOOD TODAY – A SAMPLE LEAFLET

Jane gave the following leaflet out to the children and read it through with all of them. After you have read the informed consent leaflet for children, try designing and writing such a leaflet for your own research.

Research on childhood

This leaflet has been designed to try and answer some of the questions that you might want to ask. You may show this leaflet to your parent(s)/guardian if you wish, but you do not have to do so.

What is research?

Research is a bit like being a detective. It is about investigating a particular topic and collecting evidence so that you, and others, can know more about the topic. This will help people to understand the topic better.

(Continued)

What is the research about?

This can best be answered by giving you examples of some of the things we will be thinking about: What is childhood? At what age does childhood end? What are the best things about being a child? What are the worst things about being a child? What do you like doing? What don't you like doing? What are the differences between children and adults? In what ways are children and adults similar? Are you in a hurry to grow up?

Why have you been asked to take part?

I am not a child and so I don't really know what it is like to be a child today! The best people to tell me what childhood is like today are those who are experiencing it at the moment – you! On the topic of childhood you are the expert. Your views are therefore very important to me.

What will you be doing?

Three different activities have been planned:

a. A questionnaire – this is a series of questions that ask for your thoughts on things to do with childhood. There will also be some diagrams to complete. This will be done on your own, in class. It is *not* a test. There are no right or wrong answers – it is just about what you think.
b. Designing a poster about childhood – this will be done in small groups. You will be asked to look for things at home that you might use for your poster. Each group will discuss their poster with me.
c. Talking with me about childhood – this will take place in small groups of two, three or four children. The aim of the talk will be to develop ideas and issues emerging from the questionnaires and posters.

Who else is involved in the research?

A questionnaire will be sent to your parent(s) to ask for their views about childhood. I am also looking at the newspapers, and the news on the radio and television, to see what they say about children and childhood.

Do you have to take part?

You have the choice as to whether you want to take part in each activity, but I hope that you will find it interesting and want to take part! It is an opportunity for me to learn from you and for you to put your views across.

Will anyone be told about what you say?

I will need to talk about the research with some people and I will also need to write about it, but no one (including your teacher and your parents) will ever be told who said what.

Although it is unlikely, if you do tell me anything that really worries me, then we (you and I) will need to work out what to do about it.

Thank you for reading this! If you have any other questions, then write them on the back of this leaflet and show them to me when you next see me.

(*Source*: Cox, 2005)

Using the disrespectful research methods listed on page 65, which adults would not accept, is likely to lead to poor research results. Not only is this a problem for the particular piece of research, it is also likely to reinforce negative stereotypes about children's competencies in research. Thus, the unacceptable research methods above tend to perpetuate negative myths about children in research. In the following section, respectful research practices with children are discussed.

SOCIALLY INCLUSIVE AND RESPECTFUL RELATIONSHIPS WITH CHILDREN

Listening to young children is central to ethics because:

- it acknowledges children's *right* for their views and experiences to be taken seriously about matters that affect them
- of the difference listening can make to our understanding of children's priorities, interests and concerns
- of the difference it can make to our understanding of how children feel about themselves
- listening is a vital part of establishing respectful relationships with the children we work with, and is central to the learning process.

With a clearer understanding of children's lives, parents and practitioners are able to respond to the changes in those children's lives, meet their diverse needs and improve care and services. This does not mean that in the research process children's perspectives are the sole 'voices' to be heard. Rather, listening to young children means that their 'voices', alongside those of parents and practitioners, are to be included.

According to Lancaster and Broadbent (2010: 27), 'the starting point for listening to children is to form socially inclusive relationships'. The key to inclusive and ethical social relationships is to *respect* the child and this involves granting that young child social ability and intelligence. In a respectful research relationship, the child is viewed as a person who has a valid and worthwhile perspective to offer on events that affect his or her life. In a respectful relationship, the researcher does not limit and constrain the child's potential and possibility because of that child's young age.

Respectful research relationships, based on informed consent, will go some way towards alleviating the power differences between researchers and children. However, it is important not to minimise the power held by researchers: 'The biggest ethical challenge for researchers working with children is the disparities in power and status between adults and children' (Morrow and Richards, 1996: 98). Adults researching children carry power on the basis of their age relative to children and because of the unequal nature of much research. The power that adults possess may also be related to the relationship between adult and child, such as a parent, health worker, childcare worker or teacher, in which the adult has responsibility for the child in various ways. This relationship will affect the quality and **reliability** of the evidence produced. The ways in which children may provide answers that they think a more powerful adult, such as a practitioner/researcher, wants to hear are discussed in Chapter 7.

ACTIVITY 4.2

In what ways do you hold power over the children you are carrying out research with?

Are your research questions and methods appropriate for those children?

How can your research methods challenge and question the power difference between adults and children?

How does gaining informed consent from children help to reduce the power differences between adult researchers and children?

In what other ways can you alleviate the power differences between yourself and the children?

ACTIVITY 4.3

The following questions are intended to problematise and provoke a discussion concerning the issue of gaining informed consent with children. Informed consent with children is a difficult and problematic issue, and there are no clear-cut answers to the following questions. The answers must partly be dependent on the context in which the research is being carried out.

How can the children be included in the research design?

How do we inform children about the research?

What are the ways in which informed assent can be gained with children?

How do we let children tell us that they no longer wish to participate in the research?

Do children feel they can tell us that they no longer wish to participate in the research?

How do we know that the children understand that they have the right to 'opt out' of the research if they choose?

What qualities are needed within the researcher–child relationship to allow a child the space to 'opt out' if they so choose?

Within a school context, is it possible to alleviate the power differentials between an adult researcher and a child in order to allow for greater ownership of the research by the child?

How do we close the research?

Are the research findings to be presented with the children or to the children?

Will the research make a difference to the school and the children's lives?

How can we find out if action has been taken on the research outcomes?

Alderson (2008) asks the following questions concerning informed consent:

- Do we always have to obtain parents' as well as children's consent, even for older, Year 6 children?
- Should we be barred from doing the research by parental refusals when children want to join the research?
- Is the head teacher's consent sufficient or ought we to ask every child in the school who might be observed?
- How do we research with whole classes, if one or two children object?
- How can we reduce the risk of children being coerced into joining a project?
- How can we reduce the risk of children being unwillingly excluded and silenced?

INFORMED CONSENT IS AN ONGOING PROCESS

Very young children may indicate that they like or dislike taking part in a research study in a number of different ways. Central to early years should be a commitment to listen to and respect young children's viewpoints. Informed consent, especially with young children, needs to be *continuously negotiated*. Informed consent is not a one-off event, it is a dynamic and subtle process. A child who wants to participate in the research one day, may change their mind the next day and no longer wish to participate. This right *not* to participate on a particular occasion, frustrating though it might be for the researcher, has to be respected. In case study 4.4, it can be seen how the research process and the children's participation were continuously negotiated.

NEGOTIATING ACCESS WITH GATEKEEPERS

Gatekeepers are those professionals such as nursery managers, key workers, school teachers, head teachers and parents who can literally allow you entrance to the institution to carry out the research or forbid you from doing so. Such professionals act as gatekeepers both to their institutions and to the children who are their responsibility. In terms of whether you can do your research in the institution, the gatekeepers are very powerful people, hence the importance of gaining the gatekeepers' consent and trust to carry out that research. You may also wish to interview and questionnaire the gatekeepers. So when seeking permission from gatekeepers, whether this is the nursery manager or parents, it is vital that they are provided with all relevant information about the research.

The institution may check with parents and guardians that it is acceptable to carry out the research at the nursery or school. Note that it is not a legal requirement for a school or institution to do so since they are *in loco parentis*. In practice, early childhood institutions will often act *in loco parentis* for parental permission by granting consent for the research *on behalf* of the child and the parent within the institution. However, as this chapter has consistently argued, wherever possible you should gain informed consent/assent from the children themselves as ethical best practice. This is expected in your research project. Complete disclosure of all relevant information should *always* be given to children and young people, and their informed consent sought as well as that of the gatekeepers. The institution may allow a researcher to give permission forms to the children to pass on to their parents, such as the sample letter in the box.

EXAMPLE 4.1: EMAIL LETTER SEEKING PERMISSION FROM PARENTS/GUARDIANS

Smiletown Nursery, Uptown

Dear Parent,

We have an authorised student, Helen Jones, working with us from Uptown College who wishes to carry out small-scale research with the children. She is looking at how Smiletown promotes the emotional development of the children. Such research will be valuable for the nursery since it is good to get another perspective on what we do here with the children.

As part of Helen's research, she wishes to consult with the children about what they like and dislike here; read stories with the children and do play improvisations; and do some drawing and painting with them.

Please read this letter with your child and discuss any questions that they may have. If you are happy for your child to participate in this research, please email back or print, sign and return this form to me.

Yours sincerely,
Joan Smith

I am happy for my child .... to participate in the research outlined above. Signed .... (Parent/Guardian)

─ 🔍 ──── **CASE STUDY 4.4** ──────────────────────

Helen's research was concerned with how a nursery could promote children's personal, social and emotional development. Helen chose Smiletown Nursery for her research because it had recently been designated as a centre of excellence and was therefore more amenable to research. She initially wrote to the nursery manager, identifying herself, the research's aims, and seeking permission to do the research at Smiletown Nursery (see the permission letter on page 73). The manager took the request to a subsequent staff meeting and all the staff agreed that Helen could carry out the research. They also suggested that the manager should write a letter to the parents outlining the research and that if the parents agreed they should sign and return the agreement slip at the bottom of the letter (see the letter for parents on page 70). About half the parents responded positively to the letter and returned the agreement slip.

Helen phoned the manager to arrange a meeting to discuss further the research and to listen to the manager's suggestions for this. It was agreed that she could visit the nursery for one day a week over a period of five weeks.

Together with the nursery staff, Helen explained to those children whose parents had agreed that they could participate in the research, and that she had come to the nursery to find out what the children liked and disliked at the nursery. This would help the nursery to become an even friendlier place. Some of the children said they knew about the project because their mums and dads had told them it was 'OK' to do it. Helen asked the children which activities they would like to do with her that would help her understand more about the nursery. One child suggested that they could tell her about the things they liked and disliked and another suggested that they do drawings for her. Helen said she would do both those things with the children. One child wanted to know if she could get more toys for the nursery. Subsequently, Helen and a member of staff worked with this child in a group looking through children's toy catalogues to discuss what sort of toys the children wanted to buy.

The children were told that today Helen was going to read *Blue Kangaroo* and they could then re-make the story using special finger puppets. Three children elected to work with her. Helen explained to these children that she would be using a tape recorder and showed them how it worked and that they could turn it off at any time if they wished. They then had fun recording their voices and playing with the tape recorder. Helen explained that the tape was just for her to listen to but that she may have to tell the staff about any 'difficult things' that the children told her. The children said that this was OK.

On her return visit the following week, Helen asked these three children if they wished to do a painting activity with her. Jane and Isabelle said 'no' because today they wanted to play outside with their friends. Jane and Isabelle clearly stated their preference and,

(Continued)

although disappointed, Helen respected the girls' decision to withdraw from the research activity for the day. Different children wanted to join in the painting activity with Helen. On a subsequent occasion, Jane and Isabelle agreed to participate in the research.

At the end of the research, Helen gave the nursery staff a small booklet of her findings. This booklet had been carefully discussed with her supervisor since such a feedback document needs to be sensitively written. Helen also shared verbally the main findings of her research with the children. She then listened carefully to the staff's and children's comments about her findings. She wanted to check that her interpretations of what she had seen and heard were acceptable to the children and the staff. As a thank-you present to the whole nursery, Helen bought a big drum for the children to play with. She also made individual thank-you cards on her computer for the children and the staff who had participated in the research. She gave the nursery manager a box of chocolates.

Helen was aware that not all the children would have understood what she had told them. She explained individually to the bilingual children what her research was about. Such individual explanation is critically important for some children. Helen made no assumptions about the children's participation and for each different research activity and experience their informed consent was renegotiated. She listened respectfully to their ideas about buying more toys for the nursery, and with the agreement of the nursery staff asked the children what they wanted to buy from the catalogues. The children chose more musical instruments. This process helped them see that Helen took their suggestions seriously.

GATEKEEPERS' PERMISSION LETTER

A permission letter should be sent or given to the gatekeepers. If you are a student at a college or university, the permission letter should be printed on letter-headed paper with the institution's details. All gatekeepers and participants are entitled to know who is conducting the research and where they can be contacted. The permission letter should contain the following information:

- Identity of the researcher
  - The name(s) of the researcher
  - An address and other contact details at which he or she can be contacted
  - Where appropriate, the name of the organisation under whose auspices the research is being conducted

- Information about the research
  - What the research questions are
  - Which research techniques will be used to collect evidence
  - The potential benefits that might arise from the research for the institution

- Expectations about the participants' contribution
  - What tasks the participants will do
  - How much of their time this is likely to take

- Confidentiality and the security of evidence and data collected
  - What evidence will the researcher be seeking to collect?

- What will he or she do with that evidence when it has been collected?
- Where and for how long will it be kept?
- Who will see the research report?
- How will the information be kept confidential?

The following is an example of a letter which seeks permission to carry out research in a local nursery. The letter succinctly gives details of the researcher, explains the purposes of the research, what the research participants are expected to do, the confidentiality of the research, and any possible benefits the nursery can expect to receive from the research.

EXAMPLE 4.2: LETTER SEEKING PERMISSION TO CARRY OUT RESEARCH

Uptown University College,

Uptown Road,

Uptown.

Dear Joan Smith, Manager of Smiletown Nursery,

My name is Helen Jones and I am in my final year at Uptown University College studying for my BA/BSc in Early Childhood Studies. As a prerequisite for the course, I have had my Criminal Record Bureau (CRB) clearance. As part of my final year, I have to carry out and write up a small-scale piece of research totalling 6,000 words. Smiletown Nursery has been recommended since it is a Centre of Excellence. My research topic is concerned with the ways in which nurseries promote the emotional development of children.

My research questions are focused on the diverse ways that nurseries understand and implement the emotional development of children. To collect information for my topic, I would like to make some observations of your nursery and interview you and other members of staff that you can recommend. The interviews would take approximately half an hour each. I would also hope to work with the children using stories, puppets, drawings and paintings. I will provide all paper, books and colouring materials. I would hope to be able to look at your policies as well.

I will keep you informed of how the research is going throughout the project and give you a copy of my findings on its completion. I would hope that the project would be of value to your institution in highlighting the ways in which Smiletown encourages the emotional development of children.

My independent study will be read by the university college tutors. The research will be kept confidential through anonymising the name of your institution and the research participants. I appreciate your time in reading this letter and will contact you by phone shortly to see if it is possible to meet with you in your institution to discuss the research

(Continued)

further. If you wish to get in contact with me at any time, my mobile number is 08978 456372 and my email is pj2@uptown.ac.uk.

Yours sincerely,
Helen Jones

I confirm that the above is a final-year Early Childhood Studies student undertaking an independent study as part of her assessment. The student is bound by the ethical guidelines for all Uptown research, which can be found at www.uptown/ethics.ac.uk. The research project plan has been passed by the Research Ethics Committee.

Yours sincerely
Gary Hills

Gary Hills, Early Childhood Studies Programme Director
Department of Childhood Studies, Faculty of Education
Tel: 0188 56662; Email: GaryHills@uptown.ac.uk

Researchers do not have a right to carry out their research in any institution that they wish. Remember that the gatekeepers of the institution are doing you a favour by giving you access to carry out your research. They are potentially making themselves vulnerable by allowing the research to take place, since they have no absolute guarantee, other than your word, of what you will do with the information and evidence you collect from the institution. Access to institutions has to be carefully and sensitively negotiated.

Permission to carry out your research in an institution needs to be sought at an early stage. Institutions may refuse access for a variety of reasons, including, for example, being too busy and the area you wish to investigate being too sensitive for the institution. Institutions are increasingly under inspection and surveillance from a variety of agencies and may regard your research as yet another unwelcome intrusion into their working lives. If an institution refuses you permission, for whatever reason, you will have to locate another institution or carry out your research in a different way. Equally, an institution may welcome your research as a collaborative opportunity to learn with you. They may see that your research might have benefits for their institution in some way.

Even where you know the gatekeepers, namely the head teacher or manager, they will need to be formally approached with your request to carry out some research in the institution. Thus, you may already work in an institution in which you wish to carry out your research, or you may have a relative who works in an appropriate institution, or your child might attend an institution in which you wish to carry out research. In these cases, you will have some connection with the gatekeepers of the institution and your task of gaining access will be made all the easier. However, you should still make a formal request to carry out your research.

If the manager/head teacher grants you permission to carry out research, remember that they have the right to end your research in the institution at any time. Access is not a once-and-for-all event but something that needs continual negotiation. Remember, therefore, to dress appropriately and to be polite at all times to all the participants. If you have made arrangements to make observations on a particular morning, make sure you do so. Nurseries and schools are busy places and will not look kindly on researchers who do not keep their appointments. The trust that exists in the relationship between you and the participants needs to be maintained at all costs.

'FEEDBACK' AND CLOSURE OF THE RESEARCH

It is ethically important to 'feed back' what you have learnt from the research participants. Feeding back some of your findings to the children and staff demonstrates how their views have been listened to and acknowledged by the researcher. Such feedback also needs to be carefully discussed with your supervisor prior to handing it over to the institution. Since you are a first-time researcher and your research is a small-scale study, you are probably in no position to be publicly critical of an institution. It is best not to pass judgement on the evidence that you have been provided by the institution unless specifically asked to do so. This is part of your ethical responsibilities as a researcher. If required, you can simply ask questions that the institution might want to investigate further.

Feeding back to the institution is a good opportunity to say thank you to all the staff and children for participating in the research. It is generous to give a thank-you card and perhaps a small present. You never know when you might go back to the institution! Saying thank you is important because it marks the end of the research. It is necessary for the children and staff to know that you have finished the research and are leaving. Sometimes a researcher builds up a good relationship with the children who must in turn be aware that this relationship is going to end. Equally, this is the case with some researchers who become attached to the institution and the children.

— ⌕ —— CASE STUDY 4.5 ——————————————————

After spending several weeks in a Year 2 class on her research project, Phoebe became close to the children. One child in particular had disclosed information which Phoebe had found hard to accept. Jack had told Phoebe that both his parents had died in a car crash.

'This really upset me and it took me a long time to find closure after I had carried out my project with Jack and his friends. I became very close to the children and knew a lot about them. Jack was so strong and resilient – I was in awe of his personal strength in a very difficult situation. It was hard for me to say goodbye to them at the end of the project.'

The research process in the early childhood institution needs to be marked with closure, for the benefit of both the participants and the researcher.

ETHICAL DILEMMAS ARE HARD TO RESOLVE

The identities and sets of relationships within your study will be unique. Thus, the ethical principles and dilemmas that you discuss will also be unique, set within the particular context of your study. Case study 4.6 shows how ethical issues are dependent on their context and the research questions.

In the case study, a mother initially decided to carry out some research with her son's drawings. On reflection, however, she was undecided as to whether or not this was ethically appropriate. Consider the following question as you read the example: what would you do in this mother/researcher's situation?

Since ethical dilemmas such as the one in the case study are often complex and unresolved, it is important to reflect *continuously* on the ethical issues throughout the research. There is a continual need for researchers to reflect on what they are doing and why they are doing it at every step of the research process. As part of this process, researchers should also be reflexive about how their presence affects the research process (see Chapter 7).

 CASE STUDY 4.6

A mother/researcher had decided to carry out a project on children's understandings of their ethnic identities. The researcher's son was of mixed heritage and as part of the evidence collection for her project she initially decided to use her 4-year-old son's drawings. These drawings and the associated conversations pointed towards the fact that the boy had a sophisticated understanding of his complex identities. For example, the boy had curly hair but in his drawings he would sometimes draw himself with straight hair and sometimes with curly hair. His mother noted how this change in his hairstyle was dependent on the context of the drawing. When his drawings showed him with white boys with straight hair, he chose to draw himself with straight hair. When his drawings showed him with other mixed heritage children, he drew himself with curly hair. These drawings were positively interpreted by the mother/researcher as her son's attempt to make sense of his dual identity – of being both white and black. For the mother/researcher, these drawings showed how observant and sensitive her son was of his dual heritage. She asked her son if she could put the pictures in her research project where they would be seen by her college. Her son agreed.

As the mother/researcher was finishing her research project and was ready to hand it in to the college, she reflected on the context in which her son had created the drawings. These had been made in the privacy of his home on the kitchen table with his mum. She reflected on how the knowledge her son had co-produced with her was of a private, confidential and sensitive nature. She questioned whether he would want such private knowledge to be read and possibly discussed at college. She was aware that the town they lived in was quite small and that therefore, despite anonymising the drawings, it would be possible to work out whose they were. She reflected on how, as his mother, her son would tell and show her aspects of his life which he might not tell another person, such as his teacher. She was concerned not to exploit in any way aspects of her private mother/son relationship for her professional gain as a researcher. She was anxious that as her son got older he might inter-pret the research as being exploitative of an intimate relationship.

SUMMARY

This chapter has:

- discussed the legal and social importance of listening to children's voices
- demonstrated researchers' ethical responsibilities concerning informed consent, confidentiality and child protection
- reflected on the complexity associated with gaining informed consent with
- young children and the ways in which they can be told about the research
- shown how ethical dilemmas are rarely resolved but need to be reflected on by a researcher
- discussed the importance of providing feedback to the research participants and closure for the research.

RECOMMENDED READING

Coady, M. (2010) 'Ethics in early childhood research', in G. MacNaughton, S. Rolfe and I. Siraj-Blatchford (eds), *Doing Early Childhood Research*, 2nd edition. Buckingham: Open University Press. This chapter provides a detailed and thorough overview of the history of ethics in early childhood research. It includes an insightful discussion on the cultural issues in ethical research as well as practical advice on how to submit your proposal to the ethics committee.

Kanyal, M. (ed.) (2014) *Children's Rights 0–8: Promoting Participation in Education and Care*. Oxon: David Fulton. This book provides a rich and thorough overview of the critical issues surrounding children's rights and their inclusion in research. The book is packed full of stimulating and provocative case studies which would be useful to think about in the context of your research project.

WEB LINKS

www.nfer.ac.uk/nfer/schools/developing-young-researchers/NCBguidelines.pdf – a pdf of the following document: Shaw, C., Brady, L.-M. and Davey, C. (2011) *Guidelines for Research with Children and Young People*. London: NCB.

http://childethics.com (ERIC – Ethical Research Involving Children) – a thorough website that includes a rich and detailed downloadable book on the benefits gained from including children in research.

www.ethicsguidebook.ac.uk/research-with-children-105 – The Research Ethics Guidebook is a thorough and detailed website that will carefully guide you through all of your research ethics. It is an important website for early childhood researchers as it contains a succinct, accurate and significant downloadable information sheet on issues of consent and assent with young children.

www.bera.ac.uk/researchers-resources/resources-for-researchers – this includes the 'go to' downloadable ethics code that is acknowledged to be the educational standard bearer for the educational research community.

www.eecera.org/about/ethical-code (EECERA) – a dedicated professional early childhood researcher site with a useful, accurate and recent downloadable ethics manual that focuses on young children.

REFERENCES

Alderson, P. (2008) *Young Children's Rights: Exploring Beliefs, Principles and Practice*, 2nd edition. London: Jessica Kingsley.

Cox, J. (2005) 'Childhood in crisis: Myth, reality or cause for concern? Perspectives from children, parents and the news media'. PhD thesis, Canterbury Christ Church University.

Drummond, M.J. (2002) 'Listening to children talking'. Keynote speech at NCB's Early Childhood Unit's Early Childhood Conference. Available at www.ncb.org.uk/dotpdf/open_access_2/edu_Ictc_mjdspeech_2002.pdf

Lancaster, Y. and Broadbent, V. (2010) *Listening to Young Children*, 2nd edition. Maidenhead: Coram Family and Open University Press.

Landsdown, G. (2011) 'Every Child's Right to be Heard', *Save The Children*. Available at https://www.unicef.org/french/adolescence/ files/Every_Childs_Right_to_be_Heard.pdf (accessed 14 February 2018).

Langsted, O. (1994) 'Looking at quality from the child's perspective', in P. Moss, and A. Pence (eds), *Valuing Quality in Early Childhood Services: New Approaches to Defining Quality*. London: Paul Chapman.

Malaguzzi, L. (1996) 'No Way. The Hundred is There', in *The Hundred Languages of Children*. Reggio Emilia: Reggio Children. Centro Internazionale Loris Malaguzzi, Via Bligny, 1/a, 42124 Reggio. Emilia http://zerosei.comune.re.it/

Morrow, V. and Richards, M. (1996) 'The ethics of social research with children: an overview', *Children & Society*, 10(2): 90–105.

Nuremburg Code (1949) US Holocaust Memorial Museum. Available at https://www.ushmm.org/information/exhibitions/online-exhibitions/special-focus/doctors-trial/nuremburg-code (accessed 13 February 2018).

Siraj-Blatchford, I. and Clarke, P. (2000) *Supporting Identity, Diversity and Language in the Early Years*. Buckingham: Open University Press.

United Nations (UN) (1989) *Convention on the Rights of the Child (UNCRC)*. Geneva: UN.

For additional online resources, please visit **https://study.sagepub.com/roberts-holmes4e**

5

DESIGNING YOUR RESEARCH

Figure 5.1 **The relationship between research questions and research design**

WHAT IS RESEARCH DESIGN?

Research design is concerned with your research methodology, approach and data collection methods, and the subsequent analysis of your data. The research design connects your research questions to your research data (see Figure 5.1).

Your experience, interests and reading will inform your research questions. Remember, the more specific your research questions, the more focused your research will need to be. How you write your research questions will determine your research design. If you ask open-ended type research questions, then your research design will tend to follow the qualitative approach. For example, the following research questions lend themselves to a **qualitative research** design and approach:

- Why and how do children in a nursery use their outdoor environment?
- To what extent do early childhood practitioners believe in a play-based approach to learning?

- What do early childhood practitioners understand by the term 'professional'?
- How does a nursery communicate with parents and carers?

The above four questions can be successfully answered using a qualitative design and approach, whereas the following four questions tend to lend themselves to a quantitative design and approach:

- How frequently do children use the outdoor environment?
- What is the relationship between the qualifications of nursery staff and outcomes for children?

- Do children who frequently play together show higher language development?
- Does organic food without sugar result in children's behaviour being better?

In this way, we can see that the research questions themselves will determine which research approach is used. It is useful at this point to introduce the **mixed methods** research approach which combines both qualitative and **quantitative research** approaches. Mixed methods views the above research questions from a variety of perspectives and is concerned with combining methods from the qualitative and quantitative paradigms. The mixed methods research approach takes the different perspectives and angles of the two paradigms and so is able to bridge the longstanding divide between qualitative and quantitative research approaches (see Table 5.1).

Table 5.1 The qualitative, quantitative and mixed methods research approaches

Qualitative research approach	Quantitative research approach	Mixed methods approach
Does not attempt generalisations	Attempts to generalise from findings	Generalises from quantitative data and examines in depth qualitative data
Seeks multiple truths with a variety of people's understandings and perspectives	Seeks a particular truth	Embraces a range of perspectives and viewpoints using multiple data sources
Acknowledges and works with researcher **subjectivity** and bias	Attempts researcher objectivity	Acknowledges both subjectivity and objectivity depending on data sources
Process orientated	Outcome orientated	Engages with both complexity of process and outcomes
Assumes a dynamic reality	Assumes a stable reality	Understands both change and stability simultaneously
Validity of findings are specific, local and contextual	Validity of findings dependent on their research replication by another researcher doing the same project	Uses both the specific contextual qualitative data and wider generalised quantitative data

THREE RESEARCH APPROACHES

In using a quantitative or qualitative research approach, we can understand the world and human behaviour within it. Your research questions will determine which of these you will choose to work with. It is important here that you understand what the qualitative research approach is, where it has come from and why it differs from the quantitative research approach (see Table 5.1). By doing so, you will be better able to plan and carry through your research project. Quantitative or **positivist** researchers are usually associated with numerical and statistical data collection methods and qualitative or interpretive researchers with interview data methods. Mixed methods researchers combine both qualitative and quantitative data collection methods.

A useful analogy for these two approaches of quantitative and qualitative research is that of photography. When taking pictures, a quantitative researcher will tend to take wide-angled, broad sweep and panoramic photographs. These show the entire scope of a situation without much detail. A qualitative researcher, on the other hand, tends to take close-up, detailed photographs. These show the fine detail and complex interactions going on. Mixed methods uses both together and is useful in gaining different perspectives and angles of the same thing. Such a mixed methods approach is useful in ensuring your study has **triangulation**.

QUANTITATIVE RESEARCH

Quantitative research is the traditional scientific way of seeing the world. Quantitative researchers believe that 'the truth is out there' waiting to be discovered, and tend to believe that the world is logical and obeys rational scientific laws such as the 'cause and effect' principle. It is argued that human interactions are part of the scientific laws of nature and can thus be measured and quantified in the same way as atoms and chemicals. Quantitative researchers may state a hypothesis or an assumption which they will then set out to prove as either true or false. They will also tend to use experiments and large sample sizes in order to generalise from their findings.

For quantitative researchers, if the results of a specific research project are valid, they can be replicated, or copied, by another researcher when the project is repeated. Thus, validity for quantitative researchers is not influenced by them alone and anyone else should be able to carry out the same research and produce the same results.

QUALITATIVE RESEARCH

Within the qualitative approach, it is understood that the social world is created by our shared cultural understandings of situations (Punch and Oancea, 2015). Qualitative research is based on a belief that we continually create and construct our social world by negotiating with others the *meanings* of our actions. Qualitative researchers are interested in the complexity and diversity of human interactions. In their case, people and organisations tend to be contradictory and sometimes irrational. Within an early childhood setting, the *interpretation* of events by a researcher, the children, the parents and nursery workers are all equally important. For the qualitative researcher, these multiple understandings are all equally important and the range of interpretations gives the research validity. Qualitative researchers tend not to generalise from their research and have smaller sample sizes than in quantitative research. The validity is dependent on accurately representing the voices and experiences of the research participants. The authenticity of the research participants' responses can be demonstrated by cross-checking or triangulating their responses with other people. Through this process of data triangulation, it is possible to see whether the participants' responses are consistent.

MIXED METHODS RESEARCH

Mixed methods is a powerful strategy that is increasingly used in early childhood research and combines both qualitative and quantitative approaches and methods. It produces a more complete and comprehensive understanding of the research topic than just the one approach. So, for example, combining a questionnaire with a detailed in-depth **case study** enhances the research since it combines the strengths of both approaches. Within mixed methods research, there is often movement back and forth between the different approaches and methods. For example, qualitative interviews may be carried out with early childhood teachers that inform the writing of a questionnaire. Without the initial interviews, it might be impossible to know what to include in the questionnaire. Mixed methods also helps us to understand the increasingly complex lives of families, children and early childhood settings by allowing for a range of different viewpoints and understandings.

TRIANGULATION AND RESEARCH VALIDITY

A particular strength of mixed methods research is the triangulation of different types of qualitative and quantitative data. For example, if both qualitative and quantitative data sets agree, then there is a good agreement between two different but complementary sources of data. This gives the researcher confidence in the accuracy of their findings and increases the validity of the research findings. This agreement between the different research methods can be said to have triangulated the research.

Triangulation is the research practice of comparing and combining various sources of evidence in order to reach a better understanding of the research topic. Triangulation gives research validity and makes the findings more convincing. It involves the researcher collecting a range of evidence by using a variety of research methods and gives researchers the opportunity to check out their evidence from a range of sources. It is important to try to gain different perspectives. For example, if you were interested in a teacher's practice it would be insufficient to simply ask them about their practice in an interview. You would also need to observe what they did and possibly ask for the children's perspectives on their teacher too. In this manner you would be relying on three sources of evidence:

- what the teacher told you in the interview
- your observations of what the teacher actually does
- the children's perspectives on their teacher's practice.

Gail's study on work and play in the Foundation Stage involved listening to the perspectives of the children, the teachers and the parents. She made observations of what was happening in the class and followed this up with interviews with the teachers and the children, as well as questionnairing the parents about their views on work and play in the Reception class (see Figure 5.2).

Lucy's study on domestic violence involved a large questionnaire sample as well as interviews with a range of professionals. The interviews and questionnaires provided various perspectives from a number of professions, thus providing Lucy's study with triangulation (see Figure 5.3).

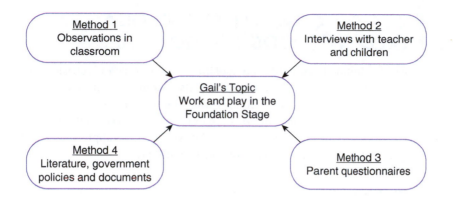

Figure 5.2 Gail's mixed methods triangulation

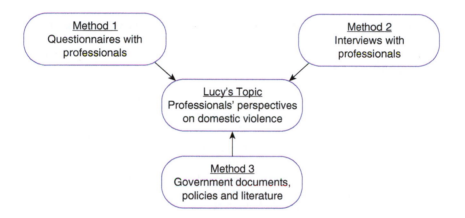

Figure 5.3 Lucy's mixed methods triangulation

ACTIVITY 5.1

Why is this triangulation of mixed methods necessary?

How can you ensure your research is triangulated?

Whose various perspectives can you include?

What other sources of evidence are available for your study?

EXAMPLES OF QUANTITATIVE, QUALITATIVE AND MIXED METHODS APPROACHES

Suppose two early childhood researchers are looking into the topic of television cartoon violence and its relationship with children, particularly its encouragement of aggressive play. In the following examples, the first study belongs within the quantitative approach, the second study within the qualitative approach and the third example the mixed methods approach. The differences between the quantitative, qualitative and mixed methods approaches (see Table 5.2) are deliberately accentuated for the purposes of understanding each.

Table 5.2 **Research topic: television violence**

Quantitative approach	Qualitative approach	Mixed methods approach
Hypothesis stated	Series of open-ended questions	Both hypothesis stated and open-ended questions
Connection between two variables assumed	No assumptions made	Some limited assumptions
Experiment devised with randomly sampled test and control groups	Purposively sampled case study described	Moves between different research methods
Children perceived as research objects to be monitored and observed	Children perceived as thinking active people whose understandings are paramount	Children understood as thinking, active participants in research process
Large representative sample size selected	Purposive sample selected through convenience sampling	Purposive sampling
Complexity of topic minimised to allow for generalisations to be made	Complexity and diversity of children's understandings sought; no generalisations to be made	Complexity engaged with
Ethical issues should be central	Ethical issues inform the research process throughout from planning to approaches to techniques	Ethical issues central
Researcher bias ignored	Researcher bias discussed	Researcher bias acknowledged and discussed

The researchers wish to understand more about cartoon violence and if this imagined violence has any detrimental effect on children's behaviour.

EXAMPLE 5.1: TELEVISION CARTOON VIOLENCE – THE QUANTITATIVE APPROACH

The hypothesis: Children who watch violent and aggressive television cartoons will role-play aggressively.

A hypothesis has been stated that there is a causal connection between two variables. These are aggressive television shows, on the one hand, and subsequent aggressive play, on the other. The hypothesis or statement suggests that there is a direct connection between these two variables. Within the quantitative approach, the researcher will set out to test whether the hypothesis or the statement is either true or false.

The researcher following the quantitative approach will devise detailed procedures before beginning the project. The project may devise an experiment possibly along the following lines. A large sample size of representative children will be located. The children will be divided into two research groups: a group exposed to aggressive television cartoons and a control group whose television viewing is filtered out for violence. Direct comparisons will be made between the experimental group and the control group of children. Other variables connected to potential violence will also be noted and removed from the experiment. The two groups of children's role-play activities will be monitored subsequently. The data collected will then be statistically analysed and interpreted and the hypothesis will be either proved correct or incorrect.

EXAMPLE 5.2: TELEVISION CARTOON VIOLENCE – THE QUALITATIVE APPROACH

Overall research study questions:

1. What do children understand by the word 'violence'?
2. To what extent do children perceive certain television shows as being violent?
3. How do children understand and make sense of these violent television shows in their games?

This time, the same research topic has been phrased as three open-ended questions. These questions have been phrased in such a way that the children's diverse perceptions and understandings of 'violence', television and role play are central to the research. The children are understood as actively engaged participants whose understandings and perceptions of the research topic will frame the research as it progresses.

Unlike the quantitative research, there is no assumption made about a connection between 'violent' television and children's aggressive play. The questions are open, tentative, and do not predict outcomes or causal connections. The first question acknowledges that the notion of violence on television is itself open to different interpretations. What may be perceived by the researcher as 'violent' may not be seen as such by the children. This opening question problematises the whole notion of the project and will lead to greater complexity and understanding of the topic.

EXAMPLE 5.3: TELEVISION CARTOON VIOLENCE – THE MIXED METHODS APPROACH

Overall research study questions:

1. Does watching violent and aggressive television cartoons encourage aggressive role-playing?
2. What do children understand by the word 'violence'?
3. How do children understand and make sense of these violent television shows in their games?

Here, both quantitative and qualitative research questions are asked, demanding a mixed methods research approach to answer them. As regards the methods, initially a small **focus group** of children may be observed engaging in free play. Any instances of aggressive play would be observed and then discussed with the children and their practitioner. This initial open-ended discussion with children and practitioners helps the researcher to understand more about children's aggressive play and any potential relationship between that and violent TV cartoons. The knowledge gained from the open-ended qualitative interviews is used to write a quantitative questionnaire that is given to all the early childhood staff and parents to complete. After analysing some of the questionnaire findings, the researcher is then able to write more interview questions for focus group discussions. In this way, the quantitative and qualitative data complements and supports each other as the researcher moves between the different approaches with mixed methods.

✎ ACTIVITY 5.2

Which of the following research topics do you think belong in the quantitative, qualitative and mixed methods approach? What are your reasons for this?

If you choose the quantitative or mixed methods approach, what would you as the researcher need to count?

With all the topics below, what possible methods might you use to collect your data and why?

What ethical issues would you need to consider?
  Research topics:

- What do Reception children at Happyland Primary School understand about the word 'friend'?
- You work for local government and need to find out if the communities in your area have heard about the SureStart programme and what they think of it.

- You want to find out the behavioural effects of watching a lot of *Pokémon* videos on a group of children compared to another group of children who do not watch *Pokémon* or any other action-type videos.
- As a nursery worker, you wish to develop boys' emotional skills through caring and looking after the soft toys and dolls in the nursery. You also want to know why the boys seem so reluctant to care for the dolls and soft toys.
- In your nursery, how many children have siblings? What age and sex are they?
- You need to find ways of getting the dads to be more active in the nursery's activities.

SAMPLING WITHIN YOUR PROJECT

Researchers sample or select particular early childhood settings, children and practitioners to study because it is practically impossible for researchers to study all early childhood settings and all children everywhere. They have to make a selection of settings, practitioners and children and this is known as **sampling**. Early childhood researchers use a variety of sampling techniques in an attempt to produce reasonably accurate findings from a selected sample. The bigger the sample size the more likely the accuracy of the findings and the greater the validity of the project. So, within a small research project with a limited sample size, it is important that you are clear about that. How this small selection is chosen is known within research as *sampling*. It is important within your research project to state how and *why* you chose your particular sample. This clarity about the sampling helps the research to achieve greater validity.

REPRESENTATIVE SAMPLING IN QUANTITATIVE LARGE-SCALE RESEARCH

Early childhood researchers who use representative samples generally have a tendency for large-scale research and quantitative research design. They use **representative sampling** because they wish to generalise their findings from the sample that they have selected to the wider population. So, for example, the large-scale early childhood Effective Provision of Pre-School Education (EPPE) project (Sylva et al., 2004) had a representative sample size of 141 early childhood centres across England. The sampling of centres was carefully carried out to produce a cross-section of both the main variety of types of early childhood settings that children attend and a cross-section of different English geographical regions. The cross-section or **stratified sampling** of the 141 early childhood centres represented the whole spectrum of early childhood provision, including playgroups, local authority nurseries, private day nurseries, nursery schools, nursery classes and integrated centres. In addition to these different representative types of setting, there were also five different geographical and socially different regions across England represented by the research, such as rural and urban areas, poor and wealthy areas and places that were a mixture of both. In each of the 141 representative early childhood settings, approximately 20 children were randomly selected, making the total research group 2,800 children. (There were also 300 children chosen who had not attended any early childhood provision.) In this way, EPPE had large-scale cross-sectional and representative sampling of six different types of early childhood provision in five different geographical areas and **random sampling** of over 3,000 children in each of the representative settings. This carefully considered representative and random sampling strategy enabled the EPPE research to make valid generalisations about the strengths and weaknesses of different types of early childhood settings across England.

PURPOSIVE SAMPLING IN SMALL-SCALE QUALITATIVE RESEARCH

Qualitative early childhood researchers tend to use some sort of deliberate or **purposive sampling**. Purposive sampling is where a researcher deliberately hand picks and chooses to sample particular settings or children to study. In other words, with purposive sampling there is no random selection or cross-sectional representative sampling. With purposive sampling, the particular setting or children may provide a good example of what that researcher is investigating. For example, in the EPPE project above, the researchers were particularly interested in the pedagogical processes that made 12 of the 141 settings highly successful. So they purposefully selected these 12 early childhood settings as case studies to further investigate what processes made these settings so outstanding. This more qualitative part of the research, known as Researching Effective Pedagogy in the Early Years (REPEY) (Siraj-Blatchford et al., 2002), deliberately selected 12 excellent case studies. Here, these 12 settings were purposefully selected to provide the researchers with in-depth knowledge about the pedagogy that led to these particular settings being excellent. With this example, it can be seen that the researchers deliberately chose settings that would help to answer their specific questions. It is interesting to note that, effectively, the EPPE and REPEY research becomes a mixed methods study: first, representative sampling was used in the quantitative EPPE research; and, second, purposive sampling was used in the REPEY qualitative research.

A further example of mixed methods research sampling might be, for example, if you were investigating the benefits of outdoor play and learning. Here, you might send a questionnaire to 10 settings that you know have good provision and you might also carry out a case study in two of the settings that have particularly good facilities. Here, you would deliberately send your questionnaire to settings that have good provision and then hand pick two nurseries which have excellent provision. Using this mixed methods approach of a quantitative survey and qualitative case studies is common. With both methods there is purposive sampling so that the researcher can find out about high-quality outdoor provision. There would be little point in researching settings that had poor outdoor provision as this would not help the researcher to answer their questions.

CONVENIENCE SAMPLING

Convenience sampling is a type of purposive sampling which, as the name suggests, is convenient for some reason for the researcher. This convenience may be because you actually work at the setting or have children at the setting or know practitioners and teachers at the setting. In each situation, you have a relationship with the particular setting and this makes gaining access for your research easier for you. It can also mean that the setting is closer to where you live and hence it is quick, cheap and easy to get to. As early childhood settings are increasingly busy places, having such a relationship with an early childhood setting may make the difference between having somewhere to research and not having a setting. It may also be that your college tutors can help you to research in particular settings. Again, this is convenience sampling to gain access to a setting for your research. Convenience sampling allows you to carry out your research in a situation in which you might otherwise not have a setting to do your research. The difficulty with convenience sampling is that it may lead to a compromise in the accuracy of your findings. Because the setting knows you and what it is your research is about, it may lead to a bias in the research findings; this is known as sample bias. Such bias, to a certain extent, can be mitigated through a process of **reflexivity** in your methodology.

Sometimes, once you have gained permission to carry out research in a particular setting or with a particular practitioner, they may then recommend other settings and practitioners to you. This is known as snowball sampling as the sample size 'snowballs' in size, with one practitioner or setting recommending another, and so on, as the sample size grows.

ACTION RESEARCH

At the heart of this research strategy is the notion of instigating change in the institution. Such change might be in the form of practice, policy and/or culture within an institution (Punch and Oancea, 2015). Action research is concerned with practically changing an issue within the working environment to improve a researcher's and their colleagues' knowledge and practice. Consequently, action research is a fairly complex and time-consuming approach to research involving the researcher's colleagues too. Action research is sometimes known as the 'practitioner as researcher' approach because the researcher and the practitioner are the same person. Action research rejects the concept of a two-stage process in which, first, research is carried out by researchers and then, in a separate second stage, the knowledge generated from the research is applied by practitioners. Instead, the two processes of action and research are integrated.

Action research is a collaborative strategy and often involves participants in the research (such as nursery workers, parents and children) in planning and carrying out the research with the researcher. Action research is thus democratic and inclusive. For small-scale first-time researchers, the nature of change in their practice and institution is likely to be small.

ACTION RESEARCH EXAMPLE

Janet wanted to ensure that the Children's Centre was inclusive so decided to invite all stakeholders in the Children's Centre to answer a series of questions concerning their practice, policies and culture. Janet arranged meetings with all her staff about inclusion and what her colleagues thought it meant and whether or not they believed their institution and practices were inclusive. Such discussions in themselves proved to be hugely informative for the staff. In addition, from these discussions the staff identified three main issues they wished to investigate further:

- Were all the nursery's children participating in all the activities the nursery provided?
- What barriers prevented some children from participating in certain activities?
- What resources were needed to ensure that participation became a reality for all children?

The staff made observations of all the children in their care over a two-month period. They then met again and discussed their findings. Several members of staff noted that the boys and girls did not play together on the 'wheelie toys' and construction activities. It was also noted that the children with physical difficulties were not using the wheelie toys. The staff agreed to discuss with the children whether and how girls and boys could play with the wheelie toys and construction equipment together. What were the children's opinions of this? What were the children's suggestions? The staff agreed to buy specialised wheelie toys for the children with physical difficulties. They then put this action plan into practice and met again two weeks later to see if this had improved their practice.

It was found that the children were more aware that boys and girls should be playing together in these activities. There were still problems however and it was decided to suggest to the children 'girl only' sessions for short periods of time and see what the children thought of this and how it would work out. The staff worked on this idea for two weeks and then met to discuss their reflections. The girl-only sessions were very popular. Girls were increasingly observed using the wheelie toys even when it was not a girls-only session.

The specialised wheelies had made a big difference for the children with physical difficulties and the staff decided to buy further specialised play equipment. It was noted that all the children enjoyed using the specialised equipment.

In the above example, it can be seen how action research develops and builds on its findings and continues to ask further questions. Action research is thus a cyclical and long-term process rather than a 'one-off' piece of research. Ideally, it should involve all stakeholders in the research process throughout.

ACTIVITY 5.3

DESIGN YOUR OWN PRACTITIONER RESEARCH

Collaboratively think of an issue/problem within your early years institution.

Draw an action research cycle involving all the issues on big sheets of paper for display.

Does your proposed action research address a practical problem?

How was the problem identified?

Who will be involved with the research and why?

Is the action research part of a continuous cycle of development, rather than a one-off project?

Is there a clear view of how the research findings will feed back directly into practice?

ACTION RESEARCH BELONGS TO YOU

Sometimes action research is referred to as 'practitioner research' because *you*, the practitioner, are at the centre of the research. One of the great things about doing *your* early years reflective practice research project is that *you* become the centre of *your* project. Action research is *insider* research. *You* are the insider and hence the central aspect of the project! As with all research, action research involves a systematic enquiry of asking questions, collecting evidence, and analysing and evaluating the findings, supported by a range of evidence.

Traditional research projects employ outsiders who are early years 'experts'. These 'experts' might be senior managers, lecturers, council policy writers, or advisors. They might come to your early years setting with agendas, ideas and questions that *they* wish to investigate. These research questions and agendas might have been written elsewhere and may or may not have relevance for you and your early years setting. These 'experts' might come to your early years setting, observe, make comments and recommendations, and then disappear. In this traditional research project, you become a participant in somebody else's research project. The exciting thing about action research is that you develop unique knowledge about yourself and your early years setting.

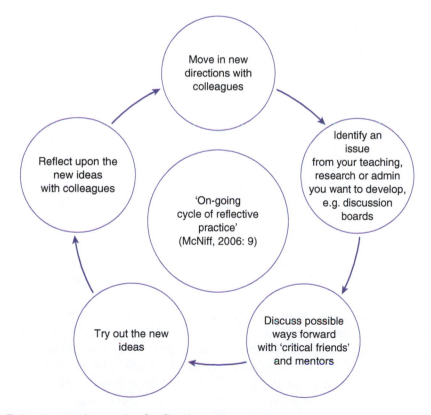

Figure 5.4 An ongoing cycle of reflective action research

THE EARLY YEARS REFLECTIVE ACTION RESEARCH CYCLE

In the early years reflective action research cycle, illustrated in Figure 5.4, the practitioner (you!) has identified an issue in your practice that you wish to investigate further. You discuss this issue with your friends and read around the issue. You then try out a new way of doing things, reflect on what was happening and then, in the light of your reflections, try a new way. The process is ongoing because when you have discovered a new way of doing things, that point itself raises new questions that you can investigate.

SIMON'S STORY OF REFLECTIVE ACTION RESEARCH

In case study 5.1, you will see that Simon's work as an early years teacher was driven by his values and principles concerning children's creativity.

— 🔍 —— CASE STUDY 5.1 ————————————————

SIMON'S STORY

I work in the early years in a large urban primary school. I am one of two Reception class teachers. I have been teaching this age group for the past five years and am concerned that less and less time is being spent on creative activities with the children. This is frustrating because when I was at college we read lots of literature about how children's creativity needs to be encouraged for their happiness and well-being. Unfortunately, there is such pressure from the rest of the school for the children to leave the early years with school-based numeracy and literacy knowledge that there is little time now for anything else! This is the problem that I identified as needing to be further explored in a reflective action research project. I framed my reflective research project around the following central research question: 'To what extent is there a lack of creativity in the early years in my primary school?'

I organised focus group discussions with early years colleagues in this school and another one a mile or so away about this issue. This was very interesting and we decided to keep a timetable and calculate exactly how much time we spent on creative work with the children each week. The discussions and the timetables provided evidence that colleagues were frustrated by the lack of time allocated to creativity in the early years. I wrote up all of this as a reflective practice research project but I wanted to do more. How could I change this situation so that I was able to work in line with my beliefs and values about young children's learning? I was very lucky as at that time there were some grants made available for teachers to make study tours to other countries. I chose Denmark as I knew that there was a lot of creativity in schools there.

Once there I talked to many early years teachers who were able to spend far more time working creatively with children. In the Danish primary school, I experienced levels of creativity amongst the children unseen in my school. On my return I shared my experiences with the whole staff. Some colleagues, including the head teacher, were very keen to develop the ideas. With the support of the head teacher, I set about a further project to encourage creativity amongst staff and children in the early years. After much discussion together, we decided to work with an 'artist in residence' at the school. The artist and subsequent reflective practice dialogue have further transformed early years understandings and beliefs concerning children's creativity and learning. The whole action research project has reinvigorated my working life and given it added meaning and purpose! (See Figure 5.5.)

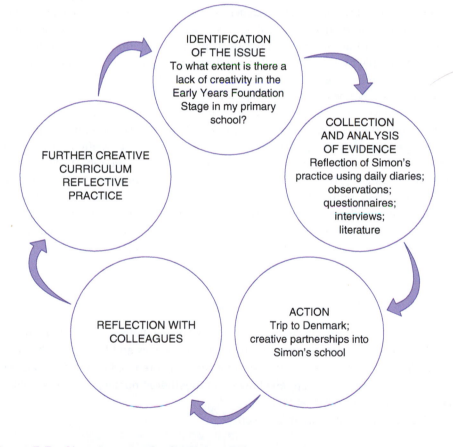

Figure 5.5   Simon's cycle of reflective practice research

As a consequence of this action research, Simon has generated theory about children's creativity, developing confidence and improved performance in the classroom. He has plenty of evidence to support his belief that creativity is important for children's well-being and classroom performance. Simon knows what he is doing and why he is doing it. He can justify his practice with his locally produced knowledge and this situated knowledge is also supported by literature. His reflective practice project is in line with his values and principles about how young children learn best. This action research project has enthused and motivated his work as an early years teacher.

CASE STUDIES

Case studies tend to have a narrowly defined focus on an individual, a family, or one or two early childhood institutions: case studies are small, and the boundaries and parameters of the research project are fairly clear, so the researcher can concentrate all their time and effort focusing on a narrow and clearly defined situation. Case studies are good for drawing out the detail and complexity of intricate social relationships within an institution. They need to be richly contextualised with plenty of 'thick' detailed description to give the reader a good sense and feel for the institution under investigation. It is important to note that generalisations concerning the research topic cannot be made from a case study.

The first example below is that of a *single* case study. This is known as an 'intrinsic' case study and can be used to study a unique or typical case (Yin, 2009: 48). The second example below is that of a *multiple* case study design: 'The evidence from multiple cases is often considered more compelling and the overall study is therefore regarded as being more robust' (Yin, 2009: 53). For a beginner researcher, the multiple case study can be comparing and contrasting two case study contexts that are similar but representative of the difference being studied. The second case study lends itself to being comparative because both the EYP and the teacher work with the same age group in the Early Years Foundation Stage and are both comparable women working in the same geographical area. Thus, they are *comparative* case studies.

EXAMPLE 5.4: SINGLE CASE STUDY

Sarah's research topic was concerned with the relationship between gender and friendships amongst a sample of ten 6-year-old children (five boys and five girls). She chose this sample of children because she knew that these children had very strong relationships based on family friendships and time spent together at nursery. Thus, the children were representative of a typical case.

Sarah's specific research questions were:

1. How do young children understand friendship?
2. How do young children understand gender?
3. Is there a relationship between gender and friendship amongst young children? If so, why is this?

Sarah's questions were centrally concerned with the subtleties and intricacies of friendship amongst young children. She wanted to find out if there was a relationship between young children's gender and their friendship. Answering such questions required the collection of delicate, sensitive and complex evidence from a small number of children. Hence, an in-depth case study was the ideal approach to answer Sarah's research questions.

The research techniques that Sarah included to answer her questions were group interviews, observations of children inside and outside the classroom, and drawings by the children of their friendships and the games they played together. Sarah also interviewed the teacher and the parents of the sample children. Such research techniques provided the level of complexity that she needed in order to answer her how and why questions.

EXAMPLE 5.5: MULTIPLE COMPARATIVE CASE STUDY

Tom, who was studying to become an early years teacher (EYT), was interested in comparing the working experiences of an EYT with those of a qualified teacher. He selected a private day nursery which employed an EYT to teach 3- to 4-year-olds and compared this person's working experiences with those of a qualified teacher working in a nursery school teaching the same age group.

Both professionals were female and of approximately the same age, and the settings were in the same district of the city, drawing on the same socio-economic mix of children. Tom's research questions were:

1. How does an EYT and a qualified teacher experience their daily working lives?
2. What is similar and different about an EYT's and a teacher's daily working lives?
3. Why are the EYT's and the teacher's daily working lives both different from and similar to one another?

As with all case studies, Tom used a wide range of data collection techniques in order to triangulate the data. He carried out a series of observations over time and several in-depth interviews with both the professionals individually and, on one occasion, together. He was also able to interview the head teacher of the nursery school and the manager of the private day nursery. Additionally, he compared and contrasted the policies and terms and conditions of employment between the EYT and the teacher.

SURVEYS

The survey tends to be a mixed methods research strategy that uses a variety of data collection methods such as questionnaires and structured interviews. Through the use of fixed interview questioning as found in structured interviews and questionnaires, the respondents in a survey are asked the same questions. Once the evidence has been collected, the researcher attempts to extract patterns and comparisons from the data. Surveys are particularly attractive for researchers who wish to statistically analyse their evidence. Surveys lend themselves to generating percentage points and graphs which clearly show the researcher's findings.

Small-scale qualitative surveys are a popular and useful early childhood research strategy and are good at producing breadth of evidence, but they can lack the depth of a case study. In the first example below, Lucy used a small-scale survey research design to answer her questions covering professional perspectives of domestic violence. In the second example, Hua Jong was interested in examining the partnership between teachers and parents at a pre-school in South China.

SMALL-SCALE SURVEY: EXAMPLE 1

Lucy wanted to investigate professional perspectives on domestic violence from a whole range of professions dealing with children: teachers, playgroup workers, social workers, domestic violence officers and family liaison officers. She was looking for evidence to analyse statistically and thus the small-scale survey strategy suited her purposes. Whilst gaining *breadth* of evidence from the survey of many different professions, Lucy lost the depth needed to answer the more complex and subtle issues within her research project. So, she combined the survey with three in-depth interviews with a range of professionals. These interviews helped to flesh out the complexity of issues raised by the 'bare bones' provided by the survey. In this way, the research became a mixed methods study with triangulated evidence.

SMALL-SCALE SURVEY: EXAMPLE 2

Hua Jong was interested in finding out more about partnerships between early childhood teachers and parents in a pre-school in South China. Hence, she conducted a small-scale survey in one particular school. Initially, Hua carried out pilot interviews with two teachers and two parents. These helped her to establish the main issues and from these pilot interviews she wrote a questionnaire and a structured interview schedule with fixed questions that focused on the parent–teacher partnership and relationship. Hua then piloted the questionnaires and the structured interviews with the two teachers and the two parents. After making all necessary amendments, she randomly distributed the questionnaires. With the agreement of the head teacher, Hua selected every third teacher and every third parent from an alphabetical register. This process ensured random sampling which added to the research's reliability. From the data collected, Hua was able to analyse the survey data and the structured questionnaire data both quantitatively and qualitatively.

BROAD AND DEEP RESEARCH

Some early childhood studies achieve breadth and **generalisability** at the same time. Figure 5.6 has plotted onto it the different research projects discussed in this chapter. Lucy's survey is a broad and general study whilst her interviews will be specific and deep, and so these are plotted in opposite corners of the diagram. Gail's and Sarah's case studies are specific but are also fairly broad in their questions. Janet's action research is also plotted in this cell because it involves a large number of people within a single institution. Aspects of a study can be plotted in various cells according to their specificity and generalisability.

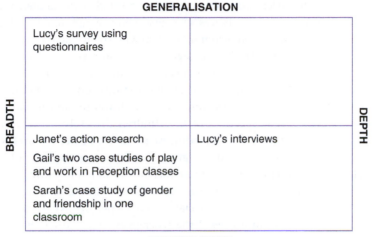

Figure 5.6 **Research can be plotted along two axes: general/specific and breadth/depth**

Source: adapted from Clough and Nutbrown (2007)

ACTIVITY 5.4

Plot the various aspects of your research study in Figure 5.6.

What aspects of your study are broad and generalisable?

What aspects of your study are specific and in-depth?

JUSTIFYING YOUR METHODS

In your research, you must justify and explain your methods as well as your choice of setting and research participants. This *justification* of your research methods shows that you understand *why* you have used certain methods and not others.

In your research, you should be able to explain:

- what your overall research questions are
- what sort of, and how much, information you need to answer your research questions
- what field questions you need to ask to get this information

- *why* you have chosen a particular setting to research
- *why* you have used certain methods and not others.

Whichever methods you decide on in order to answer your research questions, you must provide a rationale for those decisions. Providing a rationale and explanation for such research methods shows that you understand *why* you have chosen interviews rather than questionnaires and *why* you have interviewed practitioners but not children. For example, whether you decide to interview two early years students at great depth and length, or survey 50 early years students at random in their student café, you must say *why* you made these choices. Of course, you may opt for a handful of in-depth interviews *and* lots of questionnaires, but you must explain why you would do both and how your research would be improved by this. The key message here is to *justify* your research methods.

Sarah's overall research questions were concerned with the ways in which children's friendships were gendered. Specifically, her research questions centred on children's understanding of the words 'friendships', 'boys' and 'girls'. Sarah wanted to gain *insights* into the issue of friendships from the perspectives of the children themselves and was more concerned with issues of depth rather than breadth. At the heart of her research was a desire to *explore* the issue of childhood friendships rather than wanting to prove a hypothesis or statement about friendships. This complex topic was ideally suited to using interviews since they are able to elicit the sort of subtle, ambiguous and sometimes contradictory issues that arise with friendships. Sarah also wanted the class teacher's perspective on notions of childhood friendships and therefore interviewed the teacher as well. Rather than interviewing and questionnairing all 60 children in the year group, she opted for in-depth observations, interviews and drawings with 12 children and one interview with the teacher. Sarah noted subtle responses from the children when she interviewed them and was able to explore in depth some of the emotions, feelings and experiences around their friendships. Thus, interviewing was an appropriate method for Sarah to use because her overall research questions demanded insights into the children's perceptions. Using questionnaires, which would have been logistically difficult since not all the children could read and write, would not have elicited the subtle and contradictory evidence the research questions demanded.

YOUR RESEARCH PROPOSAL

There is a notable relationship between the quality of a research proposal and the subsequent quality of the research itself. All research, whether large and complex and supported by grant money or relatively small, needs to have a good clear and ethically sound research proposal. Your research proposal should clearly state: what it is that the research is trying to find out more about; why this research is worth doing; what will be learnt as a consequence of doing this research; and how you will go about collecting and analysing the data. In other words, the proposal needs to describe what will be done. The research will only be carried out after the research proposal has been approved. Writing a good research proposal involves considerable work.

The proposal is expected to demonstrate:

- what you wish to find out more about
- that your research is worthwhile

- that you are familiar with the major theoretical ideas and recent research in the area

- that you have an understanding of a particular theoretical orientation in your research area
- that you can justify your methodological approach and data collecting methods
- that you have thought about the ethical issues.

The following elements may be included in your research proposal:

1. Title
2. Abstract
3. Introduction:

    Area and topic
    Background and context
    Statement of purpose – what you hope to learn more about
    Importance of the study – why your study is important

4. Research questions

5. The literature
6. Design and methods – strategy and design:

    Sampling
    Data collection instruments and procedures
    Data analysis

7. Access and ethical considerations
8. References
9. Appendices, which may include a timetable and costs.

TITLE AND ABSTRACT

The proposed title and the abstract can be written *after* you have completed your proposal since you will have gained a clearer idea of the research through the process of writing the proposal. You will then be in a better position to write the abstract and think of a creative title.

INTRODUCTION

Within the proposal introduction, you need to show clearly the research area and topic and what the study proposes to find out more about. The introduction should also show how the study fits into existing knowledge in the topic area. In addition, your personal knowledge and experience will form part of the context of the study and can be included in the introduction. You will need to state why your research is timely and important to carry out. How will your research contribute to existing knowledge?

RESEARCH QUESTIONS

These are important and have been discussed earlier in this chapter and in Chapter 2. The key to writing good research questions is to ensure that they are specific and achievable. Make sure that your questions are viable and feasible – in other words, can you answer them within the given time frame?

THE LITERATURE

The purpose of the literature review is to provide the background to your study and identify key research in the area. You need to be able to demonstrate your understanding of research findings and issues related to your topic. Clearly, the literature review in a proposal will not be completely comprehensive. That will occur later in the study itself, but it must give an indication that you understand *how* your study fits in with the existing research and ideas in the area under investigation.

DESIGN AND METHODS

In this section, you will need to write about and justify the strategy that your study will adopt to answer the research questions. Explain why you are adopting a qualitative, quantitative or mixed methods research approach. How does your chosen approach fit with your research questions? If set within the qualitative paradigm, will your research design be a case study or case studies, a small-scale survey, an **ethnography** or action research? Explain carefully why you have chosen a particular design and how this design will help to answer your research questions. Will you carry out a pilot study? If not, why not? If a quantitative study, will your research have hypotheses and be an experiment measuring pre- and post-test variables? Whatever your research design, you must *justify* your choices.

SAMPLING

In this section, you must state what your sampling strategy will be and why. Is your study using representative sampling or purposive sampling? What is the size of your sample and how is it to be selected, and why? Remember, sampling is a key aspect for the validity of your project.

DATA COLLECTION

What are the data collection methods that you will utilise? Which methods are appropriate and feasible? How will you actually carry out the real data collection? Will your project use questionnaires and interviews and observations? If so, why?

DATA ANALYSIS

Data analysis is an important section to include in your proposal. You will need to demonstrate that you are familiar with the various analytic techniques and how you will use them. Which computer software will you use?

ETHICAL ISSUES

Ethical issues are dealt with in depth in the previous chapter. Your study should be ethically sound (that is, you should gain the informed consent of all the participants at every step of the data collection process). You should clearly state how you intend to gain access to the participants and, if appropriate, the case study settings.

REFERENCES

Finally, you will need to include a list of references for any other work cited in the proposal. The following common mistakes are made in proposal writing:

- the lack of a proper context in which to frame your research study
- not accurately presenting the contributions and references of other researchers
- a lack of focus on the research questions and not addressing the research questions.

SUMMARY

This chapter has:

- provided an overview of the major differences between the quantitative and qualitative research approaches
- evaluated the role of sampling in your research design
- examined the issues of validity and triangulation
- discussed action research, case study research and surveys
- provided an overview for your research proposal.

RECOMMENDED READING

Mukherji, P. and Albon, D. (2018) *Research Methods in Early Childhood: An Introductory Guide*, 3rd edition. London: Sage. This is a thorough methods textbook which provides a good description of the entire early childhood research process. There are clear descriptions of the various research paradigms, approaches and methods in early childhood.

Punch, K. and Oancea, A. (2015) *Introduction to Research Methods in Education*, 2nd edition. London: Sage. This reference book provides an excellent, thorough and in-depth discussion of all research approaches and methods. It is written in a user-friendly manner and illustrated with clear case studies and is recommended as a detailed reference book to further understanding of research methods.

WEB LINK

www.nfer.ac.uk/schools/developing-young-researchers/how-to-choose-your-research-methods. cfm – this is a useful and straightforward research project planning site that contains many useful tips for beginner researchers. The research process and key terms are carefully explained.

REFERENCES

Clough, P. and Nutbrown, C. (2007) *A Student's Guide to Methodology*, 2nd edition. London: Sage Publications.

McNiff, J. (2006) *All you Need to Know about Action Research*. London: Sage Publications.

Punch, K. and Oancea, A. (2015) *Introduction to Research Methods in Education*, 2nd edition. London: Sage.

Siraj-Blatchford, I., Muttock, S., Sylva, K., Gilden, R. and Bell, D., Department for Education and Skills (DfES) (2002) *Researching Effective Pedagogy in the Early Years (REPEY)*. Available at: http://dera.ioe.ac.uk/4650/1/RR356.pdf (accessed 27 June 2017).

Sylva, K., Melhuish, E., Sammons, P., Siraj-Blatchford, I. and Taggart, B. (2004) *The Effective Provision of Pre-School Education (EPPE) Project: Findings from Pre-school to End of Key Stage 1*. Available at: http://dera.ioe.ac.uk/18189/2/SSU-SF-2004-01.pdf (accessed 27 June 2017).

Yin, R.K. (2009) *Case Study Research: Design and Methods*. London: Sage Publications.

For additional online resources, please visit **https://study.sagepub.com/roberts-holmes4e**

CREATIVE LISTENING WITH YOUNG CHILDREN

LEARNING OBJECTIVES

This chapter will help you to:

- have a greater awareness of the many ways in which young children are able to express themselves
- become familiar with the connections between research and increased children's participation
- understand different ways of listening to young children
- understand how children can act as co-researchers
- understand the methods in the Mosaic approach.

DEVELOPING CULTURES OF MEANINGFUL PARTICIPATION

Genuine listening to young children's viewpoints and ideas is now at the heart of early years research and this represents a significant advance for children and their participation within early years settings. Your research should work with the ideology of listening to children.

The agenda for increasing children's participation in their services has come from three main directions. First, there is the notion that children are consumers of services, and, just as with other consumers, children's voices need to be heard too. Second, children used to be identified as part of a family or care facility and were rarely identified as a group in their own right. Children's needs and wants were interpreted by the adults around them, who spoke for them. The third main influence on children's participation has come from the UN *Convention on the Rights of the Child* (UN, 1989), discussed in the ethics chapter. The participation agenda demands a cultural shift away from working *for* children to working *with* children.

Meaningful participation requires a cultural shift by the early childhood setting from a one-off listening event to a *sustainable* participatory culture. Such a shift occurs when children's views and opinions are embedded within the principles of mutual trust and respect between children and adults. The children (and adults) need to see that their ideas are not only listened to but also *acted* on. Listening to children is only half the story. Acting on children's input is the other half. Unless action is seen to be taken, children will perhaps correctly assume that such participation is tokenistic practice.

There is a relationship between young children's well-being, including their happiness and self-respect, and a sense of connectedness to their early childhood setting when they feel that their 'voice' has been seriously listened to. Such listening is crucial to instilling in them well-being, shared values and principles, so that everyone feels understood and empowered within the early years community. Within the Children and Families Act (DfE, 2014), the Children's Commissioner's role has been increased from simply representing 'the views and interests' of children to focusing on and 'promoting and protecting' the rights of children. By creatively listening to young children, your research can actively respond to this children's rights agenda.

Good mental health and well-being, which start in the early years, partly depend on children having a sense of control, a 'voice' and decision-making powers over their learning, activities and routines. Such genuine and authentic consultation with young children can enhance children's well-being and encourage a caring, protective sense of themselves within the setting (Weare, 2015). So, participatory, inclusive and creative research can help to promote good mental health, and well-being can be promoted through creative listening. Such an understanding has recently been promoted by Public Health England (2014) and the DfE (2016), as issues around mental health and well-being become increasingly understood as important for children from the earliest age.

If, at an early age, children are encouraged to participate in decisions that affect their daily lives in their environments, and can see that such an input has real effects, then these same children are more likely to engage in participation as they get older. Engaging with children in a participatory research project may be part of a wider institutional cultural change in which inclusion and participation become embedded in the daily thinking and practice of children's environments.

What follows is a list of reasons as to why young children should be involved in participatory research projects.

PRACTICAL BENEFITS TO PARTICIPATORY RESEARCH IN EARLY CHILDHOOD SETTINGS

- Improved levels of care and education
- Improved support to ensure individuals' best interests (e.g. enhanced learning, improved health, increased opportunities for play)
- Improved experience of services (e.g. increased emotional well-being, reduced stress and feelings of insecurity)
- Improved access to and use of services
- Improved service accountability.

CITIZENSHIP AND SOCIAL INCLUSION

- Providing inclusive practice that draws in those often excluded (e.g. young children, carers, asylum seekers and disabled young children)
- Meeting expectations for children's right to participate in decisions affecting their lives
- Empowering children through being included
- Developing the skills and knowledge to be heard and fostering a deeper self-belief in the ability to create change
- Enhancing citizenship and political education, including knowledge of children's rights, structures and services
- Increasing independence and responsibility for actions
- Increasing ownership and care for services
- Improving a sense of community and belonging.

The starting point in developing such a participatory research culture is to listen to young children creatively and respectfully.

WHAT IS CREATIVE LISTENING?

In the Reggio Emilia early childhood centres of Northern Italy, children are understood as being creative, intelligent and competent. They are understood to have multiple modes of expression, including words, movement, drawing, painting, sculpture, shadow play, collage and music. These diverse modes of creative expression are known as their 'hundred languages'.

The 'Hundred Languages' poem beautifully sums up this approach:

No Way. The Hundred is There (from The Hundred Languages of Children)
The child is made of one hundred.
The child has
a hundred languages
a hundred hands
a hundred thoughts
a hundred ways of thinking
of playing, of speaking.
A hundred, always a hundred
ways of listening
of marvelling, of loving
a hundred joys
for singing and understanding
a hundred worlds
to discover
a hundred worlds to invent
a hundred worlds to dream.
The child has
a hundred languages
(and a hundred hundred hundred more)
but they steal ninety-nine.
The school and the culture
separate the head from the body.
They tell the child:

(Continued)

to think without hands

to do without head

to listen and not to speak

to understand without joy

to love and to marvel

only at Easter and Christmas.

They tell the child:

to discover the world already there

and of the hundred

they steal ninety-nine.

They tell the child:

that work and play

reality and fantasy

science and imagination

sky and earth

reason and dream

are things

that do not belong together

and thus they tell the child

that the hundred is not there.

The child says:

No way. The hundred is there.

(Loris Malaguzzi © 1996 Municipality of Reggio Emilia, Publishers Reggio Children; English trans. Lella Gandini, 1983, in Edwards, Gandini and Forman, 1995, Ablex/Greenwood Publishing Group.)

This poem is significant for early childhood researchers and practitioners since it reminds us that listening to young children need not be limited to the spoken word. Through their emphasis on the creative arts, the Reggio Emilia centres challenge the idea that visual forms of communication are somehow inferior to linguistic communication. Pressure is often applied to children to express themselves verbally, when young children might not yet have the experiences or vocabulary to do this. Young children can competently express themselves through their play and through drawings and paintings and other expressive media. Emphasising visual forms of communication potentially empowers children who are pre-verbal, have a language delay, or have English as a second language (Lancaster and Broadbent, 2010). Hence, listening to the 'voice of the child' needs to be a process which is open to the many creative ways whereby children can express their views and experiences.

Listening is:

- an active process of receiving, interpreting and responding to communication: it includes all the senses and emotions and is not limited to the spoken word
- a necessary stage in ensuring the participation of all children

- an ongoing part of tuning in to all children as individuals in their everyday lives
- sometimes part of a specific consultation about a particular entitlement, choice, event or opportunity.

Understanding listening in this way is key to providing an environment in which all children feel confident, safe and powerful, ensuring they have the time and space to express themselves in a form that suits them.

At the heart of creative listening to children is a constant raising of adult expectations of young children's abilities to communicate and express their desires and interests. The 'one hundred languages' of children *are* present and are waiting to be heard by researchers. However, early childhood researchers have to be open to these many languages in order to be able to *hear* them.

As adult researchers learn to work together with children, they may become more aware of children's strengths and competencies, and their skills are shown in clear and tangible ways. These experiences help to create a more favourable environment for dialogue and understanding. When children's participation in research takes place in an environment of mutual respect, it can lead to a change in attitudes and in the roles and capabilities of those children. This change can then lead to greater creativity, new ideas and a deeper understanding, not only of the issues under investigation but also of important issues in their community.

Sensitive and respectful researchers working in an inclusive and participatory way with young children constantly engage them in creative and innovative ways. Such researchers are well positioned to hear children's one hundred languages. The Mosaic approach has been pioneered as an effective way of listening to children's creative responses to their environment.

THE MOSAIC APPROACH

The Mosaic approach (Clark, 2017) is an integrated approach which combines the visual with the verbal. A diverse range of traditional and innovative listening techniques is put together to gain young children's views and experiences of their early childhood setting. The information collected through using the Mosaic approach can be used to make changes to the nursery.

The '**documentation**' or recording process comprises a range of evidence, including: narrative observations; consultations with the child, the key worker and the parents; children's drawings; children's photographs; and children's maps. These listening research techniques are participatory and inclusive, and the wide variety of triangulated evidence can be represented as a *mosaic* of evidence (see Figure 6.1).

There are two stages in the Mosaic approach:

- Stage 1: Children and adults gather the documentation.
- Stage 2: The information is pieced together for dialogue, reflection and interpretation.

Combining the narratives and images of the individual pieces of the mosaic helps the researcher develop a good understanding of the children's priorities.

Throughout the Mosaic approach, it is important that the children are involved in the interpretation of their photographs, drawings and tours. Within this approach, children are viewed as experts on their own lives, but they are not the only ones with this expertise. There is space within the Mosaic approach for a range of voices as well as the child's. Thus, the Mosaic approach is a way of listening which acknowledges children and adults as co-constructors of meaning. The multi-method approach brings together children's own views with those of the family and staff.

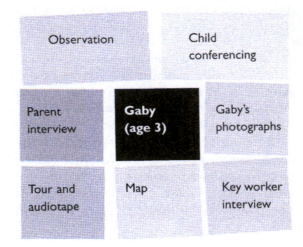

Figure 6.1   A mosaic of evidence

Source: Clark (2017)

CAMERAS AND ETHICS

Taking their own photographs provides children with the possibility of using a powerful visual language. Children using cameras to take their own pictures of their nursery setting is a relatively recent research technique. They know that photographs are enjoyable and are valued by adults, so they will tend to enjoy taking photographs. Photographs are a powerful way for children to record aspects of their daily lives. Even very young children are quite capable of taking photographs of the events and situations that affect them. These photographs can then be printed out and discussed with the children.

Some early childhood institutions increasingly own digital cameras, computers and printing facilities. The advent of inexpensive digital cameras has meant that children can see their results instantaneously on the camera itself and the subsequent computer printouts. This rapid process helps to focus children's attention on the pictures. If there is a delay of several days between taking the pictures and seeing the results, children's interest may have been lost and they may not be able to explain why they took the pictures. Disposable single-use cameras are also successful with young children because they are less expensive than digital cameras. They are also small and light enough for the children to walk around with and put in their pockets or bags to take with them.

If your research project involves you or the children taking *any* photographs within an early years setting, you *must* ensure that you have obtained permission from the manager, the practitioners, the parents and the children themselves. Ethically speaking, it is critically important to inform all the stakeholders that the project might involve taking photographs. Parents and practitioners need to know *why* children are being given cameras and what will happen to the photographs. You must therefore let the institution know how long you will keep the photographs and when you will destroy them. If you are going to take any photographs with you for your project, do make sure the children have a complete set as well. In this respect, you will need to make two complete sets of photographs.

Sometimes institutions will be willing to let you and the children take photographs as long as these do not contain people's faces. It is ethically important that if children are taking photographs of one another, they must be told to ask other children if they are happy to have their picture taken. Some may not wish to have this happen.

CHILDREN'S PHOTOGRAPHS AND WALKING TOURS

A further inclusive participatory listening technique used in the Mosaic approach is the 'walking tour' (Clark, 2017). These visual walks offer children the opportunity to share their imaginative understandings of the environment. In some ways, a walking tour is similar to an interview on the move. However, unlike some interviews, the child is in charge of the agenda and the geographical location. These walking tours can be done with individual children or in pairs and threes. At the end of the tour, children will draw maps of their nursery onto which their photographs of important places are placed. Making maps together, using the children's drawings and photographs, is an inclusive participatory activity which can reveal valuable information about the children's perspectives on their institution.

A child's photographs of their day can be used as part of their own and their family's induction process. A new child can be given a camera to take pictures of their daily routine in the nursery. They are asked to take photographs of what they like and dislike, the toys they play with, the areas of the room they use, and the outside spaces. These photographs are then placed in a book with the child's comments as to why they took the photographs, and this book is then shared with the parents with the child explaining the photographs. Such a process of documenting and recording a child's day at nursery has proved successful with parents who are excited to see what their child does.

In addition to the children's perspectives, gathered through the processes above, parents' and practitioners' perspectives can also be collected by using interviews. Parents and practitioners are extremely knowledgeable about the children and their views should be incorporated. Questions asked could include:

- What does your child enjoy doing at home?
- What do you think your child feels about being at the nursery?
- What does your child say at home about the nursery?
- What would be a good day for your child at the nursery?
- What would be a bad day for your child at the nursery?

Sometimes the child's views will echo the parents' and practitioners' and, at other times, there will be differences of opinion. This range of evidence can be documented to provide an overview of a child's experiences in an early childhood setting.

— 🔍 ———— CASE STUDY 6.1 ————————————————————

A childminder wanted to find out more about Phoebe's perceptions of being in her house and then walking to the park. Phoebe was 3 years old. The childminder explained to Phoebe that mummy and daddy wanted to know what she liked and disliked about her house and the walk to the park:

- What did Phoebe like and dislike about the house?
- What did she enjoy about going to the park and when she was in the park?

The childminder explained that together they would be sharing the photographs with Phoebe's parents. At first, Phoebe was apprehensive about making a mistake with the camera, but when the flash worked she knew that the picture had been taken. Her self-esteem and confidence visibly rose and she was soon happily taking photographs. Phoebe confidently led her childminder around the rooms she used and on the walk to the park showed her what she liked. Phoebe's comments were noted down as she took the photographs (see Figures 6.2, 6.3 and 6.4).

A visual tour by Phoebe (aged 3)
At the childminder's house

Figure 6.2   'I don't like the television 'cos it looks like an eye at me.'

Figure 6.3   'I like the books.'

Figure 6.4   'I like looking out of the window 'cos it's all out there.'

(Continued)

The childminder felt that Phoebe was in control of the visual tour and that she was positioned as the listener and learner. Giving Phoebe the camera proved successful because Phoebe was often a quiet girl with her childminder. With the camera, however, Phoebe had been given a powerful means of visual expression and the camera proved a valuable way into her thinking and understanding of her environment. As a consequence of the pictures, some changes were made around the house to accommodate Phoebe's expressions. The footstool was moved in the bathroom so that she avoided the shelf; the television was turned around; and the childminder specifically looked for Ps in books and the environment. Until Phoebe had taken the photograph of the 'P' in the street, the childminder had not appreciated that she was so observant of such rich environmental print. Such small changes in her daily routine may at first seem insignificant, but Phoebe's self-esteem was raised when she realised that the childminder was taking seriously what she had to say about her environment. Hence, her expectations of being listened to were raised and the childminder's expectations of what Phoebe observed and how she could visually express herself were also raised. Such raised expectations can lead to an enriched and more participatory relationship.

Figure 6.5   'I like those baskets 'cos they have my best toys in.'

Figure 6.6   'I don't like the shelf because I hit my head on the corner when I brush my teeth.'

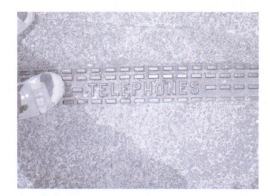

Figure 6.7   'I can see a P. That's my name!'

Figure 6.8   'I like going on Daddy's bicycle.'

Figure 6.9   'I like to hide under here and my favourite colour is yellow.'

(Continued)

Phoebe was empowered by being able to take the pictures and make a book with them. It was with great delight that she shared her book with her parents. The photographs in Figures 6.5 to 6.9 were combined with the childminder's observations and the parents' comments about what their daughter liked. This conversation confirmed that Phoebe liked to hide in places, found great delight in finding Ps for her name, and loved having books read to her. Phoebe's photographs and her perceptions were at the centre of the conversation which raised her self-esteem. The childminder was surprised at just how competent Phoebe was at using the digital camera. Her competence served as a useful reminder of how research techniques with young children need to work to children's strengths and abilities, rather than their perceived weaknesses. From such small beginnings, it is possible to see how young children's insightful comments may be used to inform changes to the existing provision or contribute to the new designs of buildings.

CHILDREN'S DRAWINGS

Children's drawings can be seen as a child's attempts to make sense of their experiences on at least three levels: cognitive, affective and linguistic. Cognitively, drawing is thought in action and is a rich way of thinking, knowing and exploring the world 'out there' via the intellect and senses. Affectively, drawing and painting are ways for children to explore and learn about their feelings. Linguistically, drawing and painting provide a space for children to develop their visual language. Drawing *is* young children's early writing and is seen as being as powerful as writing as a means of representation (Kress, 1997). In addition to the above benefits, drawing and painting are clearly vital to play, the imagination and creativity.

Many young children love to draw and paint, and will spend long periods of time concentrating on their creations. Consequently, drawings and paintings are an excellent inclusive and participatory research technique with which to listen to children. Drawings are self-initiated and spontaneously made by some children, and hence using children's drawings lends itself to 'non-invasive, non-confrontational and participatory research' (Morrow and Richards, 1996: 100). If you are going to use children's drawings in your research, you must gain **informed** assent from the children to do so (see Chapter 4). Drawings can be personal creations in which intimate and sometimes private experiences and knowledge are shared with familiar people by the children. The children may feel uncomfortable with you taking their pictures away for a wider audience than they were originally intended for by the child.

CHILDREN'S INTERPRETATIONS OF THEIR PICTURES

A potential limitation of using children's drawings and paintings in your research study is that you can all too easily impute to them your own interpretations: 'Consulting children by asking them to draw can gain illuminating evidence, but many drawings are ambiguous or vague sketches, and it is better to use them together with spoken or written comments from the child, explaining the picture' (Alderson, 2008: 200). Hence, if you are using children's drawings in your research project, it is imperative that the children are given the time and space to explain the meanings of their pictures and paintings. Researchers sometimes ask children to write a short story about their picture or to write a story and then illustrate it. However, with young children, some of whom do not yet formally write, discussing with the child what it is they are drawing *as they draw it* can be invaluable. Sometimes a young child, when asked what their picture is of, might simply reply, 'a picture'. This may be because the meaning of the picture occurs during the actual *process* of drawing or painting itself.

Hence, once the picture has been completed, the meaning is lost. In case study 6.2, it can be seen that listening to children whilst they are actively engaged in the process of drawing, painting or model-making itself may provide a good insight into what the picture represents for the child. This is because

> what the child really wants to do is to talk to himself in pictures, which suggests that the child weaves stories around the marks being made, each scribble having particular meaning dictating the story's direction so that the whole turns into a fantastical journey, a parallel for active fantasy play. (Coates, 2002: 26)

In case study 6.2, Jake re-creates a story in his drawing.

⸺ 🔍 ⸺ CASE STUDY 6.2 ⸺⸺⸺⸺⸺⸺⸺⸺⸺⸺

THE INFLUENCE OF THE MEDIA ON CHILDREN'S LIVES

The researcher used observations of play, the children's drawings and focused discussion with the children to collect her evidence with six nursery children. She wanted to know what sorts of games the children played and how these games were influenced by children's television and video stories. Specifically, in her observations the researcher listened for any television language and songs used, noted whether any television characters were adopted during role play, and how the play narratives were constructed.

In addition to observations, the children were asked to draw pictures at nursery and at home, particularly after they had been watching television. The researcher asked the children if the tape recorder could be kept on *whilst* they drew their drawings. The following is a transcript of Jake talking while drawing a picture (Figure 6.10) he made after watching the television show *Brum and the Naughty Dog*, in which a naughty dog gets stuck down a deep hole.

As Jake drew his picture, he made the following rich, detailed comments concerning his drawing:

Jake, drawing and talking: The dog's dug an either further one ... There's a tunnel here and it goes down here and there's another one here. And down here is a rabbit.

(Continued)

Researcher:	What's the rabbit doing?
Jake, drawing and talking:	There's a mole here ...
Researcher:	These are all underground creatures aren't they ...?
Jake, drawing and talking:	But the dog isn't ... the dog dug this really massive hole.
Researcher:	Why?
Jake, drawing and talking:	'Cos he wanted to ... he was getting his bones. The mole thought the dog wanted a bone so then the mole pushed a bone down the tunnel and it came out there and the dog could eat it. The mole found lots of bones and he gave them all to the dog ... he got lots and lots and lots of bones. And last of all the massive bone and that was Clifford's bone. And last of all one of Clifford's other big bones but Clifford's already eaten a bit. He's got loads of fat bones, they look like bums!!! Last of all, the longest and thinnest Clifford's been eaten through some of them ... And there was a bone that was so big it couldn't even fit through ... And last of all but not least an even bigger bone ... The mole keeps giving him bones, look here's one coming down the tunnel into his mouth ... and then he catches it.

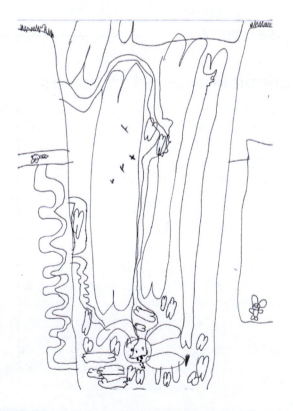

Figure 6.10 Jake's picture

Jake is clearly active in his reinterpretation of the video. The initial media plot has been creatively reworked and developed by the child in his 'storying' around the drawing. In places, the language is reflective of his book language, 'and last of all' which is said several times over. Interestingly, Jake has also used Clifford, another children's television dog character, in his intertextual story of his drawing. The rich, detailed, creative and vivid language used during the dynamic process of the drawing itself can be counterposed with the sometimes stilted, laborious and short descriptions which can occur when an adult asks a child what their picture is of.

In case study 6.3, Sarah, who used observations and focus group conversations, also used drawings to find out more about what children understand by friends.

— 🔍 — CASE STUDY 6.3 —————————————

Sarah wanted to know more about the relationship between friendship and gender. How does gender affect friendships in early childhood? One of the techniques she used was to ask the children to draw pictures of their friends and write down next to their pictures why they chose these people as their friends.

   As Jacob and Harry, Year 1 boys, told Sarah about their friendships, they drew the picture (Figure 6.11) together. Jacob did the drawings and Harry wrote the children's names. These drawings helped the boys to focus on the conversation. As they drew the pictures, they discussed why they liked having the children as friends:

Sarah: I want you to draw pictures of your friends and tell me why you like them. Only draw the people that are your special friends since it wouldn't be nice to draw people you don't like. Is it OK to tape-record this conversation as you draw? We can listen to the tape afterwards and you tell me if what you have said is OK to write down. What do you think?

Jacob: Yes, it's OK.

Harry: Yes, just the children we like to play with.

Jacob: Charlie's got quite long hair hasn't he so it goes like this.

Harry: We like playing with Charlie because he loves rockets and I like them too.

Jacob: And they blast off really really fast. We go like this ...
         Jacob gets up from the table and pretends to be a rocket 'blasting off' making rocket noises.

Jacob: I'm gonna draw someone else now. This is William because we love racing and I'm always second and we raced in our teams and my team came second.

(Continued)

Harry: Friends are fun and we love racing with them! William loves racing with us.

Sarah: Who else is your friend?

Jacob: George is and he has long hair like this. Look, that's what he's like. I like George because he plays with knight things and swords and everything and they can chop the houses down. He's got wooden ones at home which he carved with his Daddy he said. I've played with them and we went clash clash and one time he flicked mine so hard that it got stuck in the tree.

Harry: I like Alex because he plays with lots of soft toys and he brings them for Show and Tell and when it's Golden Time we can play with them in the classroom. He brings in his penguins and a big hippopotamus and because I'm a friend I can play with them. That's why we're friends.

Sarah: How do you choose your friends?

Jacob: I run up to them and I say can I play with you and they say and I say what are you playing and then I ask them whose game is it and then they say yes or no. If they say no I go and play with someone else but if they say yes then I join in the game.

Sarah: Do you play with girls at all?

Harry: No. Because they scream a lot. They chase each other and scream a lot and it makes my ears blocked.

Sarah: Do any of the girls play with you?

Harry: Most of the boys play with the boys and the girls play with the girls. Camille and Molly play with the boys though and they are in the same class.

Figure 6.11 Jack and Harry's picture

The drawings provided a powerful focus for the conversation. The drawings and conversation, Sarah's observations and the teacher's observations confirmed the gendered pattern of relationships within the Year 1 class. Sarah shared her research findings with the teacher and together they discussed ways to challenge the stereotypes boys held about girls and vice versa. In this way it can be seen that listening to the boys' conversations and their drawings encouraged curriculum development and thinking.

SUMMARY

This chapter has discussed:

- the ways in which creative listening and participation can empower children
- the Mosaic approach of creatively listening to young children
- the possibilities of children being co-researchers, setting the research agenda, and collecting and interpreting the evidence
- the importance of children interpreting their own drawings and photographs.

RECOMMENDED READING

Clark, A. (2017) *Listening to Young Children: A Guide to Understanding and Using the Mosaic Approach*, expanded 3rd edition. London: Jessica Kingsley Publishers. This excellent, rich and important groundbreaking book explores the various ways in which young children can be listened to regarding their environments. It provides innovative, creative and thorough research advice and possibilities for incorporating the multiple voices of young children.

Lancaster, Y. and Broadbent, V. (2010) *Listening to Young Children*, 2nd edition. Maidenhead: Coram Family and Open University Press. This book is a comprehensive resource to support practitioners in understanding what it means to listen and respond to what young children have to say. It gives many examples of creative ways of listening to young children that could be used as creative research data collecting methods for your early childhood research project.

WEB LINK

www.ncb.org.uk/listening-and-participation-resources – this National Children's Bureau useful and free website has links to downloadable leaflets that focus on a range of listening and participation resources written by eminent early childhood researchers.

REFERENCES

Alderson, P. (2008) *Young Children's Rights: Exploring Beliefs, Principles and Practice*, 2nd edition. London: Jessica Kingsley.

Clark, A. (2017) *Listening to Young Children: A Guide to Understanding and Using the Mosaic Approach*, expanded 3rd edition. London: Jessica Kingsley Publishers.

Clark, A. and Moss, P. (2011) *Listening to Young Children: The Mosaic Approach*. London: NCB.

Coates, E. (2002) *International Journal of Early Years Education* [to add full article details]

DfE (2014) *Young Person's Guide to the Children and Families Act 2014*. Available at: www.gov.uk/government/publications/young-persons-guide-to-the-children-and-families-act-2014 (accessed 30 June 2017).

DfE (2016) *Mental Health and Behaviour in Schools: Departmental Advice for School Staff*. Available at: www.gov.uk/government/uploads/system/uploads/attachment_data/file/508847/Mental_Health_and_Behaviour_-_advice_for_Schools_160316.pdf (accessed 30 June 2017).

Kress, G. (1997) *Before Writing: Rethinking the Paths to Literacy*. London: Routledge.

Lancaster, Y. and Broadbent, V. (2010) *Listening to Young Children*, 2nd edition. Maidenhead: Coram Family and Open University Press.

Morrow, V. and Richards, M. (1996) 'The ethics of social research with children: an overview', *Children & Society*, 10(2): 90–105.

Public Health England/NAHT (2014) *The link between pupil health and well-being and attainment*. Available at: www.gov.uk/government/publications/the-link-between-pupil-health-and-wellbeing-and-attainment (accessed 30 June 2017).

United Nations (UN) (1989) *Convention on the Rights of the Child (UNCRC)*. Geneva: UN.

Weare, K. (2015) *What Works in Promoting Social and Emotional Well-being in Schools?* Available at: www.ncb.org.uk/what-we-do/our-priorities/health-and-well-being/projects-and-programmes/partnership-well-being-and (accessed 30 June 2017).

For additional online resources, please visit **https://study.sagepub.com/roberts-holmes4e**

OBSERVATION: LOOKING AND LISTENING

LEARNING OBJECTIVES

This chapter will help you to:

- understand that observations include looking and *listening*
- have an understanding of why researchers use observations
- be aware of the problem of interpretation when carrying out observations
- know *how* to watch and listen with an open and critical mind
- begin to understand the difficulties of observation
- identify the various kinds of observations
- identify ways to record your observations
- study examples of the various kinds of observation.

WHY DO OBSERVATIONS?

Observations are one of the most frequently used forms of first-hand evidence collection that early childhood professionals make and so they are experienced in the use of observations as part of their professional working lives. This chapter builds on that experience by framing observations within the context of a research project. Early childhood researchers are continuously making observations during visits to the institutions in which they are carrying out their research. Researchers are always looking and listening for information and behaviour which will help them answer their research questions.

It is important to note that observations are frequently combined with other research methods. Thus, when carrying out interviews, drawings or questionnaires, a researcher is also making observations of the children, practitioners and parents in the setting. This chapter explores the ways in which those observations can be systematically made.

ACTIVITY 7.1

The following are some quotes from students who carried out observations for their research projects. They give a variety of reasons for doing observations.

Which of the reasons below do you think might be appropriate for you and why?

'You actually get out to see and listen to the children, the practitioners, the parents in a real-life situation.'

'It's very interesting because you can see what people actually do, rather than what they say they do!'

(Continued)

'What they say they do and what they actually do are not always the same.'

'The observations gave me a "feel" for the nursery. I was welcomed in and told that my research was needed. It felt so good.'

'Just sitting there watching and listening to all the activities for a day gave me such a good idea of the rhythm and pattern of daily life in the Reception class.'

'Observations gave me lots of ideas about what to actually ask the children later on in the interviews.'

'I got a very good understanding of the place by shadowing my mate for a week.'

'The more time I spent in the nursery, the more I understood why they do things in a certain way.'

'It was difficult because, although I tried to be "a fly on the wall", the children kept asking me questions.'

'I learnt so much just by watching and listening.'

WHAT IS OBSERVATION?

At the heart of observation is 'seeing' familiar and routine events in the early childhood setting in a new way. For example, have you ever had the experience of being on holiday and then coming back home and seeing everyday things that you always took for granted in a different way? In Britain, it is taken for granted that we drive on the left-hand side of the road, but if you have been abroad you might question this so-called normal practice. Driving on the left might feel strange for a few days. Can you think of other cultural practices that feel strange when you return home?

In a similar way, critical looking and listening in research demand that you try to make familiar everyday behaviour that seems 'normal', distant and strange. By making everyday events unfamiliar and foreign to you, you will be engaging in critical observation. Through your readings and your observations, you should try to open up and see everyday situations that you take as being normal in a different light.

INTERPRETATION

Have you ever had the experience of being at a party and then talking about it the following day with your friend? Have you noticed how you will have experienced and interpreted the same event in different ways? You were both there and probably both talked to the same people but may have come away with different perspectives and understandings of what happened. You will have to talk together to make sense of your shared experience which you have interpreted in different ways. Whether you can see the whole picture or only part of it demonstrates a dilemma for researchers; different researchers see different things. Researchers are rarely able to see the whole picture in all its complexity and only ever get a partial view. This is because early childhood researchers interpret social situations and events in different ways depending on their assumptions, beliefs and values derived from our previous experiences. Our age, gender, sexuality, ethnicity and class all help to form our experiences of life. These varied experiences then influence our perception and interpretation of events.

So 'seeing and telling it like it is' becomes highly problematic and therefore checking out other people's perspectives and interpretations of situations is critical for a researcher. This is why triangulation (the collection of different perspectives) is critical in adding to the validity of the research. With triangulated methods, the perceptions and interpretations of others, such as the children, practitioners and parents, are listened to. Acknowledging your assumptions and biases through a reflexive approach will further help to validate your observations.

BEING OPEN IN YOUR LOOKING AND LISTENING

The *way* in which you watch and listen is important. Looking and listening in research involve more than everyday looking and listening. Looking and listening in research involve doing so:

- radically
- critically
- openly
- for evidence

- for information
- for things we sometimes understand and sometimes do not understand
- to be persuaded.

Looking and listening radically and critically and in an open manner means you are prepared to suspend your assumptions and biases and try to see things from a different perspective. If you are doing so critically and openly, then you will be more ready to view your research topic in a new and different light. This might happen as you watch and listen to the events in the institution in which you are carrying out your research. Looking and listening critically do not mean that you are criticising for the sake of it, but rather, in the light of your reading on the topic, asking yourself why people are behaving in the ways that they are. All these different ways involve watching and listening to the events around you in an *active* way. This means being open as to *why* children, practitioners and parents are doing things in a different way from what you might expect.

Being aware of, listening to, and recording and reflecting on the different points of view you observe and hear are critical aspects of research observation. Indeed, observing and listening to alternative possibilities about your topic of interest might *transform* your current understanding of the topic. This involves listening, in the widest sense, to different 'voices' on a topic. Sometimes we can hold strong views on issues which research or systematic inquiry might change. Thus, opening up and listening to and watching alternative ways may lead us to question those strong beliefs and assumptions. Trying to see the world from someone else's perspective is a key aspect of research. Only when a researcher begins systematically to take into account these alternative ways of seeing the topic does mere inquisitiveness change into research.

KNOWING THE CONTEXT OF YOUR RESEARCH SETTING

One of the important ways in which researchers can open up and begin to see and hear different perspectives on their topic is to have a good understanding of the context of the institution in which they are working. Various institutions will operate in a number of ways, depending on their location and context.

ACTIVITY 7.2
OBSERVATION

The following questions will help you build up your knowledge about the wider context of the early childhood institution in which you are making your observations:

What is the socio-economic context of the neighbourhood?

Is it a well-to-do or poor or mixed neighbourhood?

Are the parents/carers professional, skilled or unskilled workers?

What is the history of the early childhood institution?

What are the sources of funding for the institution?

How many children are on the roll? What ages are they?

How many days are the children at the centre?

Which ethnicities are present in the institution?

Which languages do the children/families speak?

What is the gender balance?

How many staff are there?

What is the turnover amongst the staff?

In the following example (case study 7.1), I was interested in the issue of inclusion in a nursery. The wider context of the nursery was noted, as were the immediate entrance and my first feelings at being in the building.

 **CASE STUDY 7.1**

The nursery is surrounded by expensive new apartment blocks with balconies, land-scaped gardens and in-house leisure facilities. These have been built in the last ten years to house the nearby burgeoning financial sector workers. These apartment blocks are in 'gated communities' which have high walls and large gates serving to exclude the longstanding local community and their children who attend the local school and its attached nursery. Although the school is surrounded by such ostentatious economic wealth, 73 per cent of the pupils are entitled to free school meals, which is well above the national average and is an indication of the high unemployment and poverty experienced by the school community (Bradshaw, 2001). The local families rent flats in the nearby council tower blocks. It would seem that the local community does not benefit from the surrounding economic wealth. The head teacher confirmed this observation and stated that 'the children's poverty actually has the effect of excluding them from the local cafés, shops and restaurants. The builders even want the local park for new expensive flats.'

Once in the nursery, however, the high, cold and hard exclusionary walls that surround the school and its locale are transformed. Next to the welcome poster, translated into the children's 12 languages, is a wall covered in the photographs and names of the children and the staff in the school. The staff are representative of the different linguistic communities of the families. From floor to ceiling are large pictures that the children have recently painted. Such an entrance presents a welcome, safe and inclusive environment in stark contrast to the exclusionary feel outside the nursery's front door. A 'family room' is located off this entrance hall with armchairs and children's books, including dual-language texts and toys (Clarke and Siraj-Blatchford, 2000). Drinks facilities are also located in here. Once again, the many languages of the school are represented on the walls of the family room. This serves to include the local families. As I met the nursery head teacher, she presented me with a coffee and stated that my research on inclusion was timely and needed to be done. I felt at ease and was told that I would be introduced to all the staff and the children (Roberts-Holmes, 2001: 7).

The above broad-brush descriptive piece gives an overview of the nursery school, its immediate surroundings, and how I felt about my first impressions on being in the nursery. The unstructured and anecdotal observations are given validity by the head teacher's comments and the references to supportive literature.

UNSTRUCTURED OBSERVATIONS

In an early years setting, there will be literally hundreds of interactions going on all the time around you: practitioners talking with each other and the children, the children talking and learning with each other, parents coming and going, children moving around different activities, some children getting attention whilst others are being ignored. For a first-time researcher, this can all prove rather daunting. So what are you going to focus on?

To begin with, you can be fairly non-selective in your observations. This unfocused looking and listening are known as **unstructured observations**. In your unfocused observations, you should try to get an overall feel for the situation. Go with 'the flow' of the institution and make broad-brush notes about your feelings in your notebook. It might not always be possible to note down everything that you see, hear and feel about your research setting because your notebook might not always be to hand, hence the importance of reflecting on all that you have seen and heard in your research setting as soon as you get home. Important feelings and thoughts can be quickly lost if a note is not made of them the same day. These notes are known as anecdotal records and will provide valuable background information on the research setting. These anecdotal observations and records will record evidence of your ongoing reflective research diary.

STRUCTURED OBSERVATIONS

As you become familiar with the institution, you should progressively focus your attention on specific **structured observations**. Keeping your overall research questions in mind will help you to do so:

- What do you want to research and why?
- What is the purpose of the observation?
- What is the focus of the observation?
- How will you stay focused?

When carrying out structured observations, it is critical to be *focused* and to know exactly what you wish to look for. A good knowledge of the literature in your area will help you choose what to concentrate on. From reading in your area, you will know what is significant and important and what is not significant and not important for your study. It is imperative that you keep your overall research questions in mind when carrying out observations. If you have little time for your study, you should be asking yourself, 'How is what I am watching going to add to my research study?' Early childhood researchers use the following to help structure their observations, including tally counting, target child **observation schedules**, event sampling and target child running records, maps and diagrams and video observation.

TALLY COUNTING

As part of Katy's structured observations for her project on how nurseries support ethnic diversity, she undertook a systematic inventory of each nursery's resources. Specifically, she made a tally of the range of resources, including puzzles, books, dressing-up clothes, play food and posters on the wall, which reflected the ethnic and linguistic diversity in each of the two nurseries. This meant, for example, that she had to analyse all the books in each nursery in terms of their ethnic representation.

Figure 7.1 shows the number of books that represented diverse ethnic cultures in their pictures and storylines.

The tally chart below indicates how many of the books in the nursery setting show characters from different cultures and races ...

Characters in book are:	Number of books:
Mono-cultural (white)	ⅢⅠ ⅢⅠ ⅢⅠ ⅢⅠ ⅢⅠ ⅢⅠ ⅢⅠ ⅢⅠ ⅢⅠ III
Mono-cultural (black)	IIII
Mono-cultural (Asian)	I
Multi-cultural	ⅢⅠ ⅢⅠ ⅢⅠ ⅢⅠ ⅢⅠ ⅢⅠ ⅢⅠ ⅢⅠ ⅢⅠ ⅢⅠ
Dual-language	ⅢⅠ I 3 – Farsi + English
	3 – Somali + English

Figure 7.1   The number of books that represent diverse ethnic cultures in their pictures and storylines

OBSERVATION SCHEDULES

Observation schedules help a researcher to focus on a child or group of children or practitioner, and to attempt systematically to answer a series of specific questions (see Figures 7.2, 7.3 and 7.4).

What is the child doing?

What is the child saying?

Where is the child looking?

Who is the child looking at?

Who does the child speak to?

What does the child say?

What questions does the child ask?

Who answers the questions?

Figure 7.2   Listening and looking – a target child observation schedule

Source: Lancaster and Kirby, 2010

Who is doing what?

Who is saying what?

What do the children play with?

Who do the children play with?

Who do the children speak to?

What do the children say?

Who asks the questions?

Who answers them?

Figure 7.3   An observational schedule of a group of children playing

Source: Lancaster and Kirby, 2010

Who is the observer?				
Where does observation take place?				
Who is being observed?				
Age of child/ren:				
Purpose of observation:				
Date:				
Time	Who is present?	What is happening?	Who is the child looking at?	What is being said? Who is saying it?

Figure 7.4   An observation record sheet

(adapted from Lancaster and Kirby, 2010: 15)

ACTIVITY 7.3

Consider case study 7.2:

What were Gary's overall research questions?

What structured observation techniques did Gary use?

CASE STUDY 7.2

HOW DO 3-YEAR-OLDS SOCIALISE?

Gary's research questions were based on how 2- and 3-year-old children socially interact together. He wanted to know how some of these children who were pre-verbal made sense of their playing together. The practitioner told him to focus on a 3-year-old called Phoebe. Gary made a number of observations of Phoebe in different contexts, with the example in Figure 7.5 being made in the garden. Gary had visited the playgroup three times and was known to the parents, children and staff, and it had been agreed that he carry out these observations as part of his college study.

Gary found that the children were so interested in playing with him that it was difficult for him to write down his observations. He found that if he played with the children for 20 minutes or so and then observed them for concentrated short bursts of 10 minutes, he was more likely to be successful. The children soon realised that he was not playing anymore and left him alone.

Observation Record Sheet:
Who is the observer? Gary
Where does observation take place? Hill View Children's Centre, garden area.
Who is being observed? Phoebe
Age of child/ren: Three
Purpose of observation: Nature of social interactions that Phoebe engages in.
Date: 10.5.04

Time	Who is present?	What is happening?	Who is the child looking at?	What is being said? Who is saying it?
10.10	P and J	J is using a toy lawnmower.	P watching her.	
10.11	P and J	P gets another toy lawnmower.	J.	
10.12	P and J	Follows J round the garden.	J.	
10.14		P bumps lawnmower into me.	Me	P 'look at all the colours'.
10.15	P and J and S	P leaves lawnmower and		
10.16	S, P and J	picks up car to play with.		
10.17	S, P and J	S takes the lawnmower.	J racing P with the lawnmower.	
		P plays with toy car. S chasing J with the lawnmower.		
10.19	S, P and J, Practitioner		Practitioner gives the lawnmower to P.	P shouting at S 'it's mine, it's mine'.
		P climbs on rocking horse with wheels and races up and down wooden decking.		
10.20	S, P and J, Practitioner		Races Jane with her lawnmower.	J and P laughing together as they run.
		Phoebe gets off rocking horse and retrieves her lawnmower by pulling it from S.		
		P goes with lawnmower to the wooden decking.		

Figure 7.5 Gary's record observation sheet for Phoebe

(Continued)

In the observation (Figure 7.5), it can be seen that, even though the 3-year-olds hardly spoke, they were fully participating together in the activities. Gary noticed in his observation that Phoebe spent time looking at what other children were doing and then copied them. He noticed this in her drawing and modelling activities as well. His observations confirmed that much of young children's play is highly sociable.

EVENT SAMPLING AND RUNNING RECORDS

Sarah's research questions were concerned with the ways in which a child's gender influences their friendships. Sarah's observations were focused because she concentrated on looking at and listening to gender-influenced behaviour that she had read about. Such a focus on particular or targeted behaviour is known as event sampling. When the targeted behaviour occurred, Sarah noted it down in long-hand.

Sarah carried out a running record of the gendered interactions. A running record is a descriptive account of everything that Sarah saw and heard concerning that behaviour. In the course of one day, she noted down 25 friendship observations which centred on gendered behaviour. Sarah used a coding system for her observations to save time, rather than writing down the full names:

Running record one:

T = teacher

I = Isabelle

L = Lucy

T approaches the table and asks the girls what colour card they would like to make their litter posters on. I chooses pink and so does L. I and L pick up a pencil and begin to draw.

L: 'What are you doing?'

I: 'I am drawing a picture of a rubbish bin. See, like this!'

I shows L her drawing.

L: 'Oh yeah!'

The girls are sitting closer together. I and L get on with their respective drawings in silence for about a minute.

I: 'Can you do an "r" for me?'

I leans over and writes an 'r' on L's poster.

L: 'Oh, I didn't know how to do that because I thought you did it another way'.

I laughs and L joins in laughing too.

Running record two:

A = Anna

H = Harry

At playtime, Anna is the only girl who consistently wants to play football with the boys. Anna and Harry are sitting next to each other, reading on the carpet and looking at a Preston Pig book concerning football.

A: 'I like football and I'm really good at it.'

H: 'Yer it's true you are good but I'm the best.'

A: 'So what team do you support then?'

H: 'West Ham 'cos they're the best. What do you support?'

A: 'Gillingham and I'm gonna play for them too.'

Both of these running records of the targeted behaviour demonstrate interesting qualities about how gendered behaviour reinforces and confirms friendship. In the first observation, the two girls display compliant and positive helpful friendship (Thorne, 1993). In her research report, Sarah reflected on how her observations had changed some of the children's behaviour.

OBSERVATIONAL DIAGRAMS

Elaine's study was concerned with the use of group therapy within speech and language sessions. One of the observational techniques she used was mapping the participants during a therapy session, as shown in Figure 7.6.

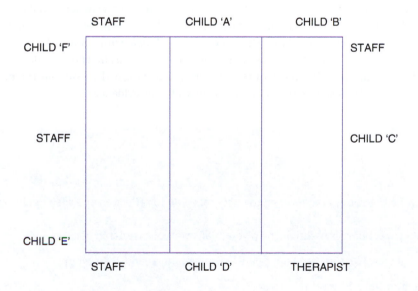

Figure 7.6 An observational diagram

Figure 7.6 is a powerful observational technique because it clearly shows how children C, D, E and F are separated from each other by the practitioners (staff) and the therapist. It is ironic that the adults themselves are acting as a barrier to the children's collaborative participation in the group therapy session.

Interestingly, in Elaine's study it was the practitioners and not the children who were affected by her presence. One of the practitioners kept leaning over to Elaine and, half jokingly, made comments such as 'I hope you didn't write that down!' and 'Don't tell them we do that when you get back to college'. Elaine assured the practitioner of the confidentiality of her study through anonymising the name of the institution. She also left a report of the study with the institution. It is important to note that professionals can often feel that they are being assessed and judged, and a researcher should be sensitive to the ways in which the observations may change those professionals' behaviour. Elaine attempted to alleviate this particular practitioner's anxiety by showing her all the observation notes at the end of each session.

PARTICIPANT OBSERVATION

In this sort of observation, a researcher actually participates and joins in with the children and the practitioners in their daily routine and activities. They become involved and included in the actual situation or event that they are researching. By experiencing the activity first hand, the researcher is able to *understand* the research topic at first hand. They are an insider because they fully participate in the event that is being studied. The depth of involvement will vary between researchers and research projects, but common to all participant observers is the large amount of time needed.

Central to good **participant observation** is spending a lot of time with the children and practitioners. The better a researcher knows the context, the practitioners, children and parents, the richer the quality of the data and evidence collected. Where a researcher is well known, they are more likely to be able to understand the detail as well as the subtleties and complexities of a situation. Developing these relationships takes a *considerable* while and so because of this a researcher should be prepared to spend large amounts of time inside and outside the research setting, developing these all-important relationships. Usually it is the case that the more time you spend in a research setting the better the quality of your evidence.

ACTIVITY 7.4
OBSERVATION CHECKLIST

The following questions are designed to encourage you to *reflect* on your use of observations:

In what ways did observations help you to answer your research questions?

Did you use structured and unstructured observations and, if so, why?

How did you know what to observe?

How did your presence affect the children?

How did the observations affect you?

What were the ethical considerations of your observations?

What were the problems and difficulties in doing the observations?

The following research (case study 7.3) arose from a concern that my 4-year-old son, Jake, might be watching too many children's videos, and thus I feared that his creativity and imagination might be suffering. This concern was transformed when I observed Jake's play after he had watched his videos. I was a participant observer in the research because I was fully engaged with my son's play, rather than a distant and removed observer.

CASE STUDY 7.3

I attempted to understand what *meaning* the video stories had for Jake in his play. As I played with Jake, I made detailed notes on the characters, toys and storylines. I reflected on how the play was influenced by the videos. I scribbled Jake's play narrative down on paper at the time Jake was playing and later transcribed and analysed it. I continued this participant observation for over three months at home and in his nursery.

The evidence that I collected from such participatory observations suggested that Jake would play with his wooden train set and 're-make' the video storylines and narratives in new and imaginative ways. The video storylines would be reworked with new engines, new situations, and other characters from different popular videos. An imaginative interweaving of plots and children's characters would emerge in this play. Thus, for example, Thomas was helped by Spiderman to ensure that Postman Pat's letters were all delivered on time! Other family members and his key worker at nursery reported that Jake's playing sometimes contained narratives from popular television shows. These different 'voices' in different contexts added validity to the findings. The mini research project pointed towards videos potentially being a *stimulus* and an important facilitator for children's creative and imaginative play (Buckingham, 1993). My initial biases and apprehensions were contradicted by the research.

As a participant observer, I was able to join in with Jake's play and gain detailed *insider* evidence and insights into his play. By recording the narrative that went with the play, I was able to note the detail, complexity and interconnectedness with the videos. At times, Jake did not like my making notes because he said 'writing stuff down is not proper playing'. Hence, I had to write the notes up later. By knowing Jake and his context so well, I was able to place his play within a rich context.

SUMMARY

This chapter has:

- discussed why researchers undertake observations
- shown you unstructured and structured ways to carry out observations

- discussed how to look and listen critically
- provided examples of various observational techniques.

RECOMMENDED READING

Palaiologou, I. (2016) *Child Observation: A Guide for Students of Early Childhood*. London: Sage. This excellent book has clear coverage of the different observational methods and is invaluable for the beginner early childhood researcher. Chapters 2, 3 and 4 explore the role of observations with young children, various observational techniques and how to analyse observations.

Rolfe, S. and Emmett, S. (2010) 'Direct observation', in G. MacNaughton, S. Rolfe and I. Siraj-Blatchford (eds), *Doing Early Childhood Research: International Perspectives on Theory and Practice*, 2nd edition. Buckingham: Open University Press. This chapter provides a very clear overview of the role of observation within early childhood education and embeds the discussion within a detailed case study which used observation.

WEB LINKS

www.earlylearninghq.org.uk/class-management/observation-and-assessment – this website contains a series of downloadable observation sheets that can be adapted for your research project.

www.youtube.com/watch?v=jNMsEEWxr_I – a useful overview of the importance of early years close observation and what to look for.

REFERENCES

Bradshaw, J. (2001) *Poverty: The Outcomes for Children*. London: Family Policy Studies Centre.

Buckingham, D. (1993) *Children Talking Television: The Making of Television Literacy*. London: Falmer.

Clarke, P. and Siraj-Blatchford, I. (2000) *Supporting Identity, Diversity and Language in the Early Years*. Buckingham: Open University Press.

Lancaster, Y. and Broadbent, V. (2010) *Listening to Young Children*, 2nd edition. Maidenhead: Coram Family and Open University Press.

Lancaster, Y.P. and Kirby, P. (2010) *Listening to Young Children* 2nd edition. London: Open University Press.

Roberts-Holmes, G. (2001) The whole family: Looking back to jump ahead, *Co-Ordinate, Journal of National Early Years Network*, Spring, issue 80.

Thorne, B. (1993) *Gender Play: Girls and Boys in School*. Buckingham: Open University Press.

For additional online resources, please visit **https://study.sagepub.com/roberts-holmes4e**

WRITING
AND USING
QUESTIONNAIRES

LEARNING OBJECTIVES

This chapter will help you to:

- develop an awareness of how and when to use questionnaires
- understand the possibilities and limitations of using questionnaires
- write questionnaires
- evaluate some examples of questionnaires.

Questionnaires are a commonly used research method in early childhood projects and can be used for a wide variety of reasons in small-scale research projects. If you wish to survey a group of early childhood professionals and parents to find out their attitudes and knowledge, then questionnaires can be a useful and relatively cheap method of rapidly collecting a wide range of views. The only way to use questionnaires with children is to read the questionnaire questions with them and make a note of their answers. Questionnaires are however generally not child friendly and so their main use is with early childhood professionals and parents. Unlike in-depth interviewing, questionnaires tend to provide a *broad* picture of early childhood professionals' experiences and views. They work through the use of standard questions which makes it possible to draw comparisons between responses. Questionnaires can be sent through the web, involve little or no personal interaction and can encourage an honesty of response as they are anonymous. However, the contradictory, ambiguous and rich detail so often elicited during interviews is unlikely to be gained using questionnaires. So a mixed methods approach would combine questionnaires with interviews and other forms of data collection such as observation and case studies.

As with all research methods, you must consider *why* you wish to use questionnaires. Questionnaires can only ever provide part of the answer to your overall research questions. They need to be used in conjunction with other research methods such as interviews, drawings and observations.

In the mixed methods represented by Figure 8.1, the interviews add 'flesh' to the 'bones' provided by the questionnaire survey. Pilot interviews can be used to gain more detailed information about a subject. The material from the pilot interviews can be used to feed into pilot questionnaires and the questionnaires themselves. Here, considerable knowledge can be built up before the questionnaires are sent out. The results from questionnaires can sometimes raise more questions than answers for both the respondent and the researcher. Some respondents write lengthy replies to questions and would be happy to talk further at length with the researcher about the issues. So, some questionnaires ask for a respondent's telephone number and email address for those willing to be contacted again by the researcher. In this way, it is possible to follow up some interesting questionnaire responses with in-depth interviewing to gain more understanding. (See Figure 8.2 for a diagram of the steps involved.)

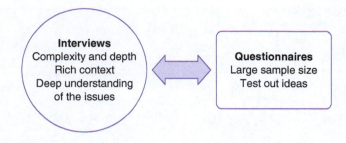

Figure 8.1   Interviews and questionnaires are complementary when used together in a mixed methods study

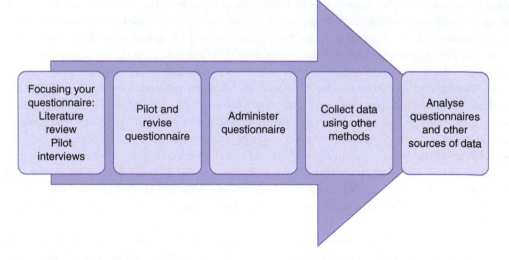

Figure 8.2   The steps involved in carrying out a small-scale questionnaire survey

WEB-BASED SURVEYS

A commonly used way to create and send questionnaires is through web-based computer programmes that specialise in internet surveys. Web-based survey companies are useful in helping you to design, distribute and analyse your early childhood questionnaires. Of course, it is also perfectly possible to design and write your own questionnaire and send it out to your known respondents via email.

Web-based questionnaires can be useful because they can make your questionnaire attractive with tailor-made images and backgrounds based on templates and examples. Delivery of the questionnaire is then made through your email contacts with respondents and of course it is also possible to alert the respondents through multiple emails and texts. Some early childhood researchers place their questionnaires on their Facebook sites and invite colleagues to respond there, whilst others use dedicated web forum pages on early childhood. Within these social media sites, all the respondents need do is click on the link in the site or email and they will be sent to the web address of the questionnaire or be directly connected to the questionnaire. Creating a professional Facebook page is a fast, efficient and cheap way to collect data for your project. For a price, commercial web-based surveys allow the data to be exported to your computer for immediate and straightforward graphical presentation of data results online in the form of graphs, percentages and PowerPoint slides.

ETHICAL ISSUES AND QUESTIONNAIRES

The issues concerning informed consent discussed in Chapter 4 are applicable if you are using questionnaires. As part of your ethical responsibility, you must gain informed consent from the appropriate gatekeepers, such as head teachers and nursery managers. It may be important for the respondents to know that their questionnaires will be anonymous – they might then give more honest responses. Self-completion questionnaires can clearly only be used by literate older children and adults. Questionnaires should only be used as prompts for conversations with the children. Furthermore, even with older children researchers cannot assume that young people will attach the same understanding to the questions used.

ACTIVITY 8.1

What are your research questions?

What sort of – and how much – information do you need in order to answer your research questions?

What does a questionnaire add to your research study?

How can you justify using a questionnaire?

What will you learn about your research topic by using questionnaires?

What other research methods will you use? Why?

In case study 8.1, Lucy discusses *why* she chooses to use questionnaires with the professionals in her sample. Her questionnaire sample was not made up of a representative sample of participants as it used purposive sampling. Through the use of her personal contacts, her Facebook friends and by reading Ofsted websites, she 'handpicked' the institutions and contacted the people she wished to survey. Lucy used her college-based questionnaire service and Facebook. She sent out her questionnaire to 70 potential respondents by email and alerted her 50 or so early childhood Facebook contacts to her dedicated early childhood research Facebook page.

─ 🔍 ──── **CASE STUDY 8.1** ─────────────────

The Uptown University College,
Uptown Road,
Uptown.

Email: Lucy@uptownuni.com

Mobile: 07790 – 675423

Professional's Questionnaire: mental health and well-being

Please state your profession ....

Q1) In your professional capacity have you had contact with or been approached by a child over concerns of mental health and well-being?
(Please tick appropriate box)

Yes: ☐   No: ☐

Q2) Were you able to listen to and support their concerns?
(Please tick appropriate box)

Yes: ☐   No: ☐   Never been approached: ☐

Q2a) If yes to question 2 were you then able to address these concerns?
(Please tick appropriate box)

Yes: ☐   No: ☐   If No, why? ....

Q3) If yes, to question 2a – To what degree did you feel successful?
(Please tick appropriate box)

| Very Successful | Successful | Adequately | Unsuccessful | Very Unsuccessful |

Other ....

Q4) Do you feel it is your place to answer questions on the issue of mental health and well-being?

If yes, why? ....
If no, why? ....

Q5) Is there a designated member of your organisation who is responsible for dealing with the issue of mental health and well-being?
(Please tick appropriate box)

Yes: ☐   No: ☐   Unsure: ☐

If yes, who ....

Q6) If yes to Question 5 – What action can the designated person take?

....
....

Q7) In some schools recently there have been initiatives (Hackney & Westminster) to address mental health and well-being through PSHE (citizenship). Do you have any knowledge of similar practices in your area?
(Please tick appropriate box)

Yes: ☐   No: ☐   Don't know: ☐

Q8) Do you think it is appropriate to include the issue of mental health and well-being within the National Curriculum in primary schools?
(Please tick appropriate box)

Yes: ☐   No: ☐   Unsure: ☐

Q9) When would it be appropriate to introduce the subject of mental health and well-being into the School Curriculum?
(Please tick appropriate box)

| 4–7 Years | 7–9 Years | 9–11 Years | Secondary Education | Not Appropriate |

Q10) Do you think issues with mental health and well-being could be prevented or reduced through education in primary schools?
(Please tick appropriate box)

Yes: ☐   No: ☐   Unsure: ☐

Thank you very much for taking the time to fill out this questionnaire, it is much appreciated, please feel free to attach additional sheets and add any other comments.

Figure 8.3 Questionnaire

As you read this case study, list all the things which Lucy did *before* she sent out her questionnaires.

Lucy's research on mental health and well-being was centrally concerned with a comparison of attitudes between the different professionals: teachers, nursery workers, social workers and mental health professionals. She wanted to compare their attitudes on whether they felt early years in schools should educate children about mental health and well-being issues. She also wanted to gain an overall impression as to each profession's feelings in this area. Lucy decided that a questionnaire survey was suited to revealing the general feelings of each profession. She opted to follow up some of the questionnaires with one-to-one interviews to clarify and further discuss the issues emerging from the generalised questionnaire responses.

After reading widely in the area and informally discussing the issues with friends and colleagues, Lucy piloted her questionnaire (Figure 8.3) with her friends and colleagues at college. Her 'critical friends' were helpful in providing comments. Using web-based templates, Lucy made several versions on her computer, cutting out and simplifying questions where necessary, and wrote various explanations as to how to complete it until she was happy that the questionnaire was likely to be successful. She also ensured that the questionnaire was well presented, not too long, and avoided asking personal and insensitive questions. She then emailed out her questionnaire to her contacts and friends in primary schools and placed the link to the questionnaire on her Facebook page and invited her professional friends to the page. Such personal contact ensured a very high response rate for Lucy.

CASE STUDY 8.2

Ruth's study concerned female nursery workers' perceptions of working with male colleagues in two all-female staffed nurseries.

At a staff meeting, Ruth explained that she wanted to know more about the attitudes of female staff and the possible barriers that men faced in working in nurseries. She asked for the staff's opinions on methods and they suggested surveying the staff with questionnaires and follow-up interviews. Subsequently, Ruth wrote and handed out questionnaires with sealable envelopes to all of the staff. Due to the sensitive nature of the topic, Ruth decided to place a home-made 'postbox' in the staffroom, for completed questionnaires to be posted in their envelopes. This postbox ensured anonymity because Ruth did not know who the questionnaires were from and, because of the ease of 'posting' in the staffroom, she obtained a high response rate. Ruth found that the questionnaire stimulated so much interest that nearly all the respondents were happy to discuss further the issues raised by it.

WRITING YOUR QUESTIONNAIRE

In order to write your questionnaire successfully, you will need to be absolutely clear about what your research is concerned with and what it is exactly you wish to find out. There is no space on a questionnaire for ambiguity or vagueness. Being too long is probably the major reason why people do not complete questionnaires. Two sides of A4 paper should be sufficient for most questionnaires and the web-based surveys provide examples of short questionnaires.

Below is a list of points to bear in mind when writing your questionnaire:

- At the top you should write a short explanation/rationale for the questionnaire if this is not already included in a separate covering letter.
- Include a statement concerning the anonymity of the respondent.
- Is the appearance and layout attractive, clear and straightforward?
- Is the language simple?
- Have you avoided leading questions (e.g. 'Do you agree that …?')?
- Are the questions short, clear and unambiguous?
- Is the technical jargon at a minimum?
- Do your questions go from easiest to most difficult?
- Have you thanked the respondents at the end?

TYPES OF QUESTION

Using a questionnaire, carried out with early childhood studies students, Figure 8.4 demonstrates five types of questions that you can write.

Types of questions include:

- making a list
- a closed question, Yes/No answer
- agree/disagree with a statement
- choosing from a list of options
- placing reasons in a rank order
- open-ended questions.

When you come to write your questionnaire, it would be a good idea to include a variety, though not necessarily all, of these types of questions to keep respondents interested in your survey. Utilising such questions can also generate various forms of evidence which you can subsequently use.

WRITING A LIKERT SCALE QUESTIONNAIRE

This is a common form of questionnaire and can be successfully used to measure people's attitudes:

1. *Write down a list of statements* that are significant and important to the respondents in your topic area. These statements can be identified from your reading in the area and informal discussions with the respondents themselves. The statements should be written as both a positive and a negative and there should be approximately

the same number of positive and negative statements.

2. *Categorise the responses* by having five fixed-alternative expressions that are labelled as follows: agree strongly; agree; unsure; disagree; disagree strongly.

3. *Ask a number of respondents* to complete the Likert scale questionnaire.

Student Motivations for Joining the Early Childhood Studies Degree

I am interested in the diverse reasons for students doing the Early Childhood Studies degree course. Your responses will provide Course Tutors with knowledge about why you are studying for the degree, which will help us to understand your needs better! This is an anonymous questionnaire so please try to answer honestly!

Male   Female   Please circle

Age:

[A list]
Please list 3 issues which motivated you to study for the Early Childhood Studies Degree.

1.

2.

3.

[A closed question Yes/No answer]
Was Early Childhood Studies your first choice of degree? *Please tick*

Yes: ☐   No: ☐

If no, what did you wish to study?

[Agree/disagree with a statement (the Likert scale)]
Generally speaking I am happy to be studying for the Early Childhood Studies degree.
Please circle ONE.

Definitely agree   Agree to some extent   Disagree

[Rank order]
From the following list of reasons as to why you initially chose to do the Early Childhood Studies degree, choose the THREE which you feel are most appropriate to you.

1 = strongest reason   2 = second strongest reason   3 = third strongest reason

Employment opportunities after graduation are good.
The only course I could get on to.
I want to work with children.
I want to help the country to meet the need for Early Childhood workers.
I'm not sure what I want to do yet, so the course gives me some time to think.
Working with children is an interesting and worthwhile job.

[Open-ended questions]
What work do you wish to do when you leave University with your Early Childhood Studies degree?
Is there anything else you wish to say concerning your reasons for studying the Early Childhood Studies degree?

Many thanks indeed for your help.

Figure 8.4   Student motivation questionnaire

— 🔍 —— **CASE STUDY 8.3** ————————————————

USING THE LIKERT SCALE QUESTIONNAIRE

Jane emailed approximately 80 early years teachers (EYTs) in her local authority with a link to a Likert scale questionnaire on her Facebook page (see Figure 8.5). This resulted in a 60 per cent response rate. She wanted to find out more about the extent to which early years teachers were able to lead learning in their settings. Jane knew that the EYTs were busy professionals and unlikely to complete a lengthy questionnaire, and so she compiled the following straightforward and easy-to-use Likert questionnaire. In addition to the Likert scale, Jane included some questions which enabled her to contextualise the EYT qualification. She was then able to follow up these questionnaires by asking a

---

Early Years Teacher Status Research Project

Dear Early Years Teacher,

We would like to know your comments and views about your role as an Early Years Teacher (EYT) in your setting. EYTs are considered to be important in raising the quality of early years provision. They are expected to act as 'change agents' to improve practice, and lead practice in the early years. I would like to explore this with you by inviting you to complete the attached questionnaire in which you will be given an opportunity to reflect on your role as an EYT.

Completing this questionnaire will help us to widen our understanding of EYTs. Your information will be analysed and treated in confidence. You and your setting will NOT be identifiable in the results. We ask for your name and setting information so that we might potentially contact you by telephone or email to ask you further questions.

Please ensure that you return your questionnaire to us by Friday February 12th.

POST: A.N. Other, University of Poppleton

EMAIL: a.n.other@poppleton.ac.uk

We look forward to reading your views.

With many thanks and best wishes,

A.N. Other

If you wish to ask for any further information, please email us or call me on 07983 234 567.

Name:

Name of setting:

Email address:

Contextual information about you and your setting – please tick or put a cross in the box

1. Type of early years setting in which you work:

Private daycare	
Primary school early years	
Children's Centre	
Sessional daycare	
Childminder	
Nursery school	

2. Qualifications on entry to EYT:

Degree with subject Early Years/Early Childhood	
Foundation degree in Early Years	
Degree in Education	
Another subject (not early years) degree	
Masters degree	
Other	

3. Have you gained new employment since achieving EYT?

Yes	
No	

4. With the following statements, please indicate your preference with a cross or tick and explain your answers in further detail.

Statement	Strongly Agree	Agree	Not Sure	Disagree	Strongly Disagree
1. My role as an EYT is not important					

Statement	Strongly Agree	Agree	Not Sure	Disagree	Strongly Disagree
2. My role as an EYT is clear to me					

Statement	Strongly Agree	Agree	Not Sure	Disagree	Strongly Disagree
3. My role as an EYT is unclear to my colleagues					

(Continued)

Statement	Strongly Agree	Agree	Not Sure	Disagree	Strongly Disagree
4. I am supported in my role as an EYT in my setting					

Statement	Strongly Agree	Agree	Not Sure	Disagree	Strongly Disagree
5. I am not supported in my role as an EYT in other contexts					

Statement	Strongly Agree	Agree	Not Sure	Disagree	Strongly Disagree
6. I am able to lead learning in my setting					

Statement	Strongly Agree	Agree	Not Sure	Disagree	Strongly Disagree
7. I am not able to implement change in my setting					

Statement	Strongly Agree	Agree	Not Sure	Disagree	Strongly Disagree
8. I am able to reflect on my leadership practices					

Statement	Strongly Agree	Agree	Not Sure	Disagree	Strongly Disagree
9. My professional development needs are not being met					

10. In this space please feel free to let me know anything else about being an EYT.

Thank you very much for completing this questionnaire.

Figure 8.5 A Likert scale questionnaire

random sample of the EYTs to further expand on why they had ticked particular statements. She chose to follow up the questionnaire with six of the EYTs in a focus group setting when they met for their monthly network meeting. This mixed methods approach to her research helped to produce triangulated and valid research.

SUMMARY

This chapter has:

- developed your understanding of the various uses of questionnaires
- demonstrated the different ways in which you can write questionnaires
- reviewed the way in which questionnaires can form part of triangulation.

RECOMMENDED READING

Denscombe, M. (2014) *The Good Research Guide*, 5th edition. Maidenhead: Open University Press. Chapter 1 of this user-friendly introductory guide to research focuses on the survey approach, whilst Chapter 11 is concerned with writing questionnaires. Both chapters are recommended as together they offer the novice researcher a good foundation in the use of the survey design and the questionnaire method.

Siraj-Blatchford, I. (2010) 'Surveys and questionnaires: an evaluative case study', in G. MacNaughton, S. Rolfe and I. Siraj-Blatchford (eds), *Doing Early Childhood Research: International Perspectives on Theory and Practice*, 2nd edition. Buckingham: Open University Press. This chapter provides an interesting discussion on ways to use questionnaires combined with interviews in a small-scale survey. The chapter includes a useful overview of the research design and sampling issues to be addressed when carrying out a small-scale survey.

WEB LINKS

www.surveymonkey.co.uk/mp/education-surveys
www.smartsurvey.co.uk/questionnaire-design
www.questionpro.com/sample-survey-questionnaire.html

The above is a list of the more popular commercial web-based survey companies, but some colleges and universities subscribe to web-based questionnaire services so it is advisable to ask your tutor as you may be able to access such a service for free.

For additional online resources, please visit **https://study.sagepub.com/roberts-holmes4e**

INTERVIEWING CHILDREN AND ADULTS

TYPES OF INTERVIEW

There are various sorts of interviews, including:

- structured interviews
- semi-structured interviews

- focus group interviews
- email interviews.

STRUCTURED INTERVIEWS

Structured interviews are similar to questionnaires in that the interviewer has a set of predetermined questions which are asked in a set order. This set of predetermined fixed questions, known as the interview schedule or guide, determines and dominates the structure of a rigid and structured interview. Using the mixed methods of questionnaires and interviews, then closely following a structured interview schedule, which is largely based on the questionnaire, is a useful approach because using the same questions in the questionnaire and the structured interview ensures triangulated data. In the following structured interview schedule, the researcher's topic was early years phonics in the first year of primary school. Before writing the questions, the researcher carried out a literature search on the use of phonics and grouping and her questions led from this literature search. The researcher used the same questions in both her questionnaire, which was sent to 20 teachers, and in her interviews with three teachers. This cross-referencing of the same questions using two different methods enabled the questionnaire and interview data to be clearly triangulated.

STRUCTURED INTERVIEW SCHEDULE: PHONICS IN YEAR ONE

1. Does your early years setting teach phonics in any way?
2. If so, why is this?
3. Does your setting use a particular phonics scheme and, if so, why?
4. Does the phonics scheme encourage particular pedagogic practices such as grouping and, if so, what are they?
5. What are the processes by which a child's phonics group is decided?
6. Who decides on a child's phonics and when? What evidence is used?
7. To what extent is it possible for children to move between phonics groups? Are any changes monitored at all?

SEMI-STRUCTURED INTERVIEWS

By contrast, in a semi-structured and unstructured interview, the focus is shifted away from the researcher towards the issues and interests of the research participant. In a semi-structured interview, the interview schedule or guide is flexible and can vary depending on how the interview is going. The role of the interviewer is one of facilitator and enabler who encourages the research participant to 'speak their mind' on issues. The interviewer 'gets the ball rolling' and thereafter listens carefully, asking for a development of issues as they arise during the conversation. Where necessary, the interviewer will ask a direct question but the direction and content of the interview will stem from the research participant as the interviewer listens carefully. Semi-structured and unstructured interviews are on a continuum, and an interview will slide back and forth between them. In a semi-structured or unstructured interview, there is more space for the respondent to elaborate on the points that are important to them. During semi-structured interviews, the researcher usually has an **interview guide** or schedule which simply lists the points which the researcher wants to cover, but, unlike the interview schedule, the guide is not fixed and predetermined. The interview guide is simply five or six open-ended questions that will guide the interview rather than dictate the structure and content of it. Such an open-ended research guide allows the researcher to keep the interview focused on the research subject and, at the same time, to be sufficiently flexible to allow for the interview to change tack if the respondent wants the discussion to go in a different direction. What follows is Sarah's interview guide concerning friendship with a group of children:

- How do you make friends with other people?
- What sort of people do you choose to be your friend?
- What makes a good friend?
- What sorts of things do you like best about your friends?
- What makes a bad friend?
- What sorts of things do bad friends do?

ACTIVITY 9.1

Now try writing an interview guide for your research topic. Remember to base such a guide on the literature, your feelings, and your observations of the research setting. Pilot this interview guide with your friends/family/children to see how it works. Remember to check whether you have left out any important questions or avenues for discussion.

PROBING IN SEMI-STRUCTURED INTERVIEWS

A key skill that interviewers need to develop is the ability to know how and when to 'probe' respondents for more information. Such **probing** helps to elaborate, confirm and clarify what a respondent is saying and requires the researcher to be familiar with the issues being discussed and aware of what is important and needs further clarification. This is where a researcher's background reading and research about the setting are important.

Probing-type questions include the following:

- I don't quite understand, can you explain a bit more?
- Can you give me an example of what you have just said?
- What do you mean?
- Can you give me more details about that?

In your pilot interview with your friends and family, make sure you use some probing-type questions. Can you think of any more of these?

KEY SKILLS OF INTERVIEWING

Despite the fact that interviewing is rooted in a skill that researchers already possess, namely the ability to hold a conversation, good research interviewing is much more demanding than it might at first appear:

- The issue of informed consent (see Chapter 4) places a responsibility on you as the researcher. You have a responsibility to tell a respondent to stop if they begin to share material which may force you to break confidentiality due to child protection issues.
- Knowledge of the subject, gained from a thorough literature review and knowledge of your specific research setting, will contribute to your knowledge of the setting and help to produce a more focused and informed discussion.
- Empathy, respect and sensitivity are essential for conducting a good interview with a respondent. You will need the ability to 'read' the social dynamics and not just the content. If a respondent shows signs of feeling uncomfortable with an issue, you will need to move on.
- You must remain non-judgemental during the interview. Researchers can sometimes hold strong opinions about a subject, and respondents' viewpoints might be different. Your job is to listen respectfully to respondents' viewpoints, not try to persuade them of your feelings about the topic.

In the following interview guides about gender, can you see how the first interview guide is prejudiced and will lead the children to think in certain ways?

Interview 1

Are your best friends boys or girls? Why?

Why do girls like reading and writing and boys like playing football?

Why do girls play quietly and boys play noisily?

Why do girls like dolls and boys like guns?

In this first interview guide, the questions are not neutral and objective but prejudiced and stereotypical. The questions are *leading* the children along a certain train of thought. They confirm stereotypes and invite the children to expand on such stereotypical notions. These prejudices will be picked up by the children and other stereotypical examples found. The children may wish to challenge such stereotyped notions but the questions are so biased that they may feel unable to do so.

> *Interview 2*
>
> Can you tell me what you think about girls and boys?
>
> Are girls and boys the same?
>
> What do you think about boys?
>
> What do you think about girls?
>
> What did you think about the video?

In this second interview guide, the questions are much more open-ended and neutral. They are not leading questions and as such they allow for a range of possible answers. They are sufficiently open to allow for responses which challenge gender stereotypes.

FOCUS GROUPS
FOCUS GROUP CONVERSATIONS WITH CHILDREN

Children can feel intimidated by a one-to-one interview with a researcher, especially if they are not familiar with that researcher. Being familiar with the children you hope to interview or consult with is crucial to the success of the interview. Such relationships are important when interviewing children because they are not used to their opinions and experiences being sought by unknown adults. Because of this, many researchers will spend a week or two working voluntarily and making observations in a setting before attempting to interview the children there. During this period, a researcher can get to know the children and hopefully build up their trust.

However, it is important to choose the group of children carefully because some might dominate others and shy children might not talk for fear of reprisal or ridicule when they do. Here again, the choice of children for a focus group discussion critically depends on a researcher's familiarity with the children. Sometimes the key worker or teacher can help a researcher choose which children to put in a focus group or the children themselves can choose who they want in their group. So, for example, a child who wants to participate in the research might be chosen and that child will then be asked to nominate two or three of their friends. Very often, young children are so good at talking amongst themselves that the researcher just has to start with an open question and let the children respond!

Central to the success that can be gained from group conversations is the potential for the power dynamics between the researcher and the children to be shifted in favour of the latter. Thus, group interviews where a small group of friends – perhaps three or four – are interviewed together tend to make children more relaxed and comfortable. They tend to enjoy social situations and activities and therefore focus groups with other children appeal to their sociability. Moreover, children can listen to each other's ideas in focus groups and encourage each other in the process of articulating their thoughts. In mixed-age groups, younger children can gain encouragement to talk from the older children. As a result, focus groups tend to be successful in terms of generating discussions amongst children. In successful focus groups, the researcher can take on the role of discussion facilitator rather than being 'the interviewer' with a set of specific questions.

In terms of their strengths, focus groups:

- provide an opportunity to work collaboratively – they encourage interaction between children
- can be empowering for individuals by building confidence
- may give children space to raise the issues that they want to discuss
- recognise children as experts in their own settings
- give insights into young children's shared understandings of everyday life
- generate new ideas through the interactions between all members of the group
- focus on having conversations rather than question-and-answer interviews
- are familiar to children.

However, focus groups may have the following limitations:

- It can be difficult to identify the individual from the group view.
- Individuals can be influenced by others in a group situation.

FOCUS GROUP DISCUSSIONS AND CHILD-CENTRED ACTIVITIES

When interviewing children, some researchers have found it best to do so whilst the children are actually engaged in an activity. Through the use of books, prompts, games, puppets, soft toys and dolls, researchers can choose to engage in a gentle child-centred discussion with the children. Using children's drawings and their photographs encourages the interview to be child-centred and focused. Using children's drawings and photographs in the process of listening to children is discussed in the following chapter. Using child-centred structured activities helps to avoid adults dominating the interview. Utilising such child-centred activities helps to avoid 'test questioning', where the children are expected to produce the 'correct' response for the researcher. Children are often expected to guess what an adult wants them to do and say, and interviewing can be seen by children as an extension of this adult-dominated process. Through the use of participatory research techniques, a researcher respectfully attempts to enter the world with which a child is familiar. Such socially inclusive ways of working with children encourage high-quality and valid research interviews.

For example, Sarah, who was researching children's friendships, interviewed groups of three and four children whilst sitting on the carpet with them. Sitting on this carpeted floor in the cosy book corner, out of earshot of the teacher, provided a convivial context for the children to talk. She started by reading the children the book *Something Else* (Cave, 2011) and encouraged them to think about how Something made friends with Something Else. On another occasion, she used the class teddy bear, pretending that he was new to the class and wanted to make friends with the children. What sort of things should teddy do to make friends in the classroom? The discussion was further personalised by encouraging the children to bring in their favourite teddy bears and soft animals and talk about how they would make friends if they were new to the classroom.

Sarah situated herself as an 'inexpert' on friendships, particularly friendships between children, because she was not a child. She stated that she did not know very much about children at all, but was very interested in them and wanted to learn all she could about children and friendships. Being familiar with the children, reading with them, playing games with soft toys and positioning herself as an inexpert, all encouraged the children to talk.

Sarah read *Something Else* and discussed it with the children. The children then 'introduced' their soft toys and said how they made friends with other toys. Once they had begun to talk freely and with confidence about friendship, Sarah asked the children about their friendships in school:

Sarah: I want to know more about your friendships. I don't really know anything about how children make friendships. Can you help me, please, by telling me what things make a good friend?

Jake: I like a friend that is kind to me and helps me with my work and I like a friend that plays football with me. All the boys play football, Jack, Lewis ...

Lewis: Yeah, yeah, I like a friend that plays football with me and plays with me in the playground.

Jane: I like a friend that plays with me. I like it when my friends come to my house for a party.

Lewis: Yeah, yeah ... I like a friend that comes to my house and plays with my remote control car.

Sarah: Good for you! You are so clever at making friends. I bet you have so many friends. Thank you for telling me all that. I'm beginning to learn about how to make friends now. You're just great. Now, listen, can you tell me the sort of things that you don't like friends to do?

Jane: I don't like a friend who puts me down or is mean to me. I don't like a friend that bosses me about.

Jake: I don't like a friend that hits me. You have to tell before they run to the teacher and tell a lie! Tell them that you hit them!!! I don't like people who do that.

Lewis: Billy isn't my friend when he loses a game. He always loses and hits other people and then ... and then hits me too.

FOCUS GROUP DISCUSSIONS WITH ADULTS

All the above arguments regarding focus group discussions or interviews with children apply to focus group discussions with adults too. Focus group discussions can be good at eliciting a large amount of information from a small group. This is because the respondents listen to, respond to and develop each other's arguments as would be the case in a 'real-life' discussion. Focus group discussions can build confidence amongst practitioners to develop their thinking together and thus can give rise to far richer data than single interviews.

In a group discussion on assessment (Activity 9.2), a researcher, E, was a teacher in the school where the four respondents were also employed:

Participant A: Nursery nurse
Participant B: Teaching assistant, full-time
Participant C: Nursery teacher
Participant D: Teaching assistant, part-time
Participant E: Researcher

ACTIVITY 9.2

As you read through the following excerpt from the group interview, think about the following questions:

- Does the researcher ask open or closed questions?
- Are the questions 'leading' or 'biased' in any way?
- Why does the researcher occasionally summarise and reflect the discussion back to the respondents?
- How does the researcher further probe the respondents?
- To what extent do the respondents listen to each other?
- Do the respondents build on each other's ideas and thinking?

E: At the moment the way we do assessment is based on observations. So, we do Post-it notes, we do photographs, and we take samples of work. So what do you think of the way that we do it: is it good enough, is it comprehensive, does it capture the children's learning, is it an efficient way of working?

A: I think sometimes the narratives are a bit like lip service because I sometimes do a narrative and I think 'What has this taught me about the child?' I got nothing from it. Me and B often discuss them together, what would be the next steps, what do we do with this observation. You know it doesn't tell me anything about the child. So I do sometimes think, the whole point of a narrative is to look holistically at the child but I think we need to plan our observations or I need to plan, how I feel, I need to plan my observations better, think more about what I am wanting to get out of that observation, rather than just following the child around for the sake of ... I don't know.

E: So when you are doing a narrative are you thinking 'Well, what's this all for? What's the point of it?'

A: When I read it back or I write it out again, like if I want to do it neater, I think this doesn't tell me anything about the child. Now I don't know, is that down to my observation skills or is that down to ... ?

E: Is there a difference with children, do you find?

A: Mmm, mmm.

E: Do you think, some children when you observe them you get more from them?

B: Exactly, we get more information for the children who are very talkative and socialise with the other children, and if it's quiet children we are struggling because of how to motivate them or how to socialise to get some more information from that child.

E: OK, so narratives are not the best form for those particular children.

B: Exactly, but my point of view is for me I find observation narrative easy because I can see the other development area which I haven't covered from that child. So the best thing

(Continued)

about the narrative, often we can see how much that child is in the one place and not improving in the other development areas.

E: You think there's an advantage of the narrative over the short observations, the Post-it notes and things like that?

B: Yeah, yeah.

E: Yes, I guess, what do you think C?

C: Well, I find the narrative observation useful. It's the way you incorporate in your assessment, the narrative observations. But I think your question was more directed to children who are quiet and how can we improve assessment. We, because we are very fortunate we are a team. We don't do a summative assessment as a team with the children probably due to the number of children we are working with, but the assessment should be with all our points of view and gathering all the evidence, and the other thing probably that we don't do is include the child in their own assessment. So there will be two things, do the things that we are doing and probably they will teach us how to improve our assessment, how we don't look at things from the point of view and how we could do other areas of development with the child. So I think we are lacking of that in our assessment. Including the child in their own assessment, asking other children who have their own language, to help us to communicate and with that child to get the best, because I think with assessment, we should be looking at the full child's potential when we do the assessment, it's not only what we look at and we will see as individual professionals, it's about what the child sees and the other professionals.

A: Are we valuing parents then enough? We talk about the learning journeys, are we really, really, really valuing their opinions, their contributions because we're, I don't know, maybe we're not putting ourselves out enough? I know it's hard at times.

E: So how can we do that then with parents? There are two questions really, how can we do that with parents and how can we involve the child more in their own assessment?

A: I think we can't do one without the other.

E: How can we do that?

A: Well, let the learning journeys go home.

E: In a manageable way. So, you think the learning journeys should go home?

D: We had the video cameras going home. That's a way of assessing.

A: We're not allowed to let the learning journeys go home.

C: Is that a proper assessment because we considered that a child has achieved an objective when it's able to apply that learning in any context? So sometimes we see children performing better at home and they are not performing here at the same level. So you know...

A: But it's about evidence, can you tick a box?

C: We should have an agreement about what we should include in assessment, because if you really embedded the learning you should be able to do exactly the same what you do at home in a rich environment that the child feels secure in like here.

A: Does that mean that they don't feel secure at nursery then?

C: Well, you know, I think our nursery has very positive characteristics but one of them is for a quiet child...

A: It's quite overwhelming, isn't it?

C: It's about the amount of children that we have, and even the way that we distribute the furniture and the way we organise things. You know a quiet child often, very often, you know, that's what I think personally, gets lost in this environment.

CHILDREN AS RESEARCHERS

The power dynamics between adults and children are perhaps the major difficulty that faces researchers. Such power dynamics can be a barrier to the collection of high-quality evidence from young children. A possible way to overcome this difficulty is to invite other children to be researchers themselves. Thus, children interview other children. This 'child-to-child' technique has been pioneered in international development as a tool for conveying information to children as well as to discover their views. The thinking behind this method is that children, because of their 'inside knowledge', might be able to ask more relevant questions than adults. Older children can also work with younger children to elicit their views. The closeness in age helps to alleviate some of the power differentials and the older children's interests, perceptions and understandings might be that much closer to the younger children's than the best attempts by adults could ever be. In case study 9.1, older children were co-researchers and made a video for younger children to help them settle into Reception class. The case study shows that the research had real and unanticipated outcomes.

— 🔍 —— CASE STUDY 9.1 ————————————————

Debbie was interested in involving Year 1 children as co-researchers in a project. She explained that her research was concerned with finding out more about things. She showed the children a range of methods to collect people's views of things, including asking people about issues using a tape recorder and videoing events. The children practised using tape recorders to record conversations and also practised making videos of their favourite things in the classroom.

Debbie invited a group of children to work with her on a project of the children's own choosing. The children suggested several projects that they wished to research, including:

- litter
- things they liked and disliked about the school
- being helpful and kind to others
- setting up a school sweet shop.

(Continued)

Debbie gave the children time to discuss the different topics amongst themselves, make drawings and develop their ideas. The main issues which came out of these discussions concerned things the children liked and disliked about the school. Figure 9.1 shows Sam's picture of things he liked and disliked about school.

Figure 9.1   Sam's picture

The first picture shows Rainbow class ''cos that's where you do loads of art and art is really good'; the second picture shows 'the big grassy field where we can play and run around lots'; the third picture shows 'eating a nice lunch with corn and sausages'; the fourth picture shows 'the really bad thing, teachers shouting. Lots of people shout when they're cross and it makes my ears hurt in the class'. The fifth picture shows how good and bad children's names are written on the board and 'my name is never written on the board for either'.

With Debbie's support, it was decided to combine two topics: 'things we like and do not like' and 'being helpful and kind to others'. Some of the children talked about how they had younger siblings and friends in the nursery attached to the primary school and how they wanted to help these younger children settle into the Reception class the following term. This was thought to be a good idea and, in particular, it was decided to show them the things they might really enjoy, such as the big grassy field, 'Golden Time' for playing, doing art, and the lunches. The children thought they should not tell the nursery children about the shouting because it might scare them. However, Debbie noted the children's concerns about teachers shouting.

The Year 1 children decided that the best way to show the young children what the Big School was like was to make a video of important things. Debbie suggested that they did not yet know what was important for the younger children. So the children decided that they would go and talk to the younger children about the things they wanted to know more about in joining Big School. When they knew what the younger children wanted to know, they would make a 'helpful and kind video'.

The Year 1 children and Debbie visited the nursery children and told them that they wanted to help them settle into Reception class next term. Some of the nursery children did not wish to participate in the project but the children who had older siblings as Year 1 researchers were keen to join in. In pairs, the older children asked groups of younger children what they knew about Big School and what scared them. The Year 1 children used tape recorders to record the conversations.

On their return to the classroom, the Year 1 children listened to the tapes and, together with Debbie, identified the following themes which the younger children wanted to know more about. The main issues which came out of these discussions were:

- Where were the toilets?
- What friends would there be?
- Where did children eat and what food was there?
- What did people do at playtime?
- Would the older children hurt the nursery children?

In groups of three, the children used the digital video camera to film where the toilets were located; that you had to ask for school dinners or a packed lunch at register time; that you had to line up for dinner or sit at tables for the packed lunch; that you could play on the big grassy field when it was not raining, or the hard playground when it was wet, and they filmed all the games that were played in the playground. The video also showed that if you did not have a friend, you could ask the dinner ladies for help. The children talked about 'some nasty big children who hurt people'. Debbie realised that the school did not have an anti-bullying policy. Debbie promised the children that she would look into this and let the children know what the school's response was. (Subsequently, the school did produce an anti-bullying policy.)

With the children, Debbie edited the video on the computer and the children then took it to the nursery to show it to the nursery children. The nursery children were delighted to see the video and it gave rise to a lot more questions being asked which the Year 1 children were happy to answer.

The above project was successful because Debbie played the role of facilitator of the research and the children were the co-researchers. The children were the initiators of the ideas, collected the evidence and produced a video to help the nursery children. Producing the video showed the children that their ideas and the knowledge they had generated were important. Debbie reported that the Year 1 children's self-confidence and self-esteem had visibly risen as a result of making the video. The fact that the school had listened to and taken on board the children's concerns around bullying in the playground, and had subsequently acted to produce an anti-bullying policy, had further enhanced the children's self-confidence. The video the Year 1 children made concerned the toilets, lunch and playing on the grass. The development of the anti-bullying policy represented a significant step towards acting on the children's interests and concerns. Perhaps sometime in the near future, Sam's frustration with 'teachers shouting' might also be addressed. It is important to remember that young children's increased participation in their institutions, through such a research project as described above, is a process. Working with children as fellow researchers is a major step in the direction of participatory and inclusive research with young children.

A WIDE DIVERSITY OF INTERVIEW RESPONDENTS

It is crucial to ensure that you have interviewed as wide a variety of the children and adults in your setting as possible. Hence, boys and girls and ethnic minority children and disabled children should be represented in your sample of children and adults. Hearing this diversity of children's and adults 'voices' adds to the validity of your research by ensuring that no one voice, for example boys' or girls', will dominate the evidence you generate. It is also vital to remember that children do not form a homogeneous group, rather that their voices are many and varied. This can depend on a child's gender, class, ethnicity, mother tongue, location and physical ability. Your research should attempt to reflect this rich diversity of children's experiences and opinions, and in this way it will prove all the more convincing to the reader.

DIGITALLY RECORDING YOUR INTERVIEWS

Digitally recording your interviews on your smartphone, rather than writing them down, is an important research interview habit to develop because it allows you to do your main job, that is, active *listening*. Recording allows you the space and time to focus on your discussions with the research participants. Not writing everything down, which is almost impossible anyway, frees you up to concentrate and think about the issues arising in each interview. These may go off in different directions from those you would expect, and so you will need to focus on the content and on asking appropriate questions rather than your handwriting.

Occasionally, a person may not wish the interview to be recorded, usually because they are unsure of what you will do with the recording. This situation might arise where the interviewer and the research participant do not know each other. You must inform the research participants as to what you intend to do with the recording (see Chapter 4 on informed consent). Children tend to enjoy hearing their voices on the recorder and will gladly sit and listen to the recording with you. This provides a good opportunity to check with the children the meaning of the conversation and to clarify any points you may be unclear about. This adds to the validity of the evidence you collect.

Always check that you are completely familiar with the workings of the digital recorder and that you have sufficient battery time! Transcribing the recordings, or writing them up, takes a long time. A half hour of recorded interview can take two hours to transcribe. It is best to play the entire recording and listen carefully to the ideas and themes arising in the interview and note these down. Once you have an overall understanding of the whole, it is much easier to replay parts of this and select exactly what you need. This process of listening and re-listening to the recording, and transcribing key parts word for word, gives a level of understanding and analysis that is difficult to achieve with jotted-down notes. With the recording, you get *everything* that was said, and with its transcription you will be able to carry out a thorough and reflective analysis.

ACTIVITY 9.3
FOCUS GROUP INTERVIEWING

In groups of three or four, carry out a focus group interview. This will help you pilot your interview guide and practise using the digital recorder. For approximately 10 minutes, each student will need to use their interview guide questions with their colleagues. Use the recorder to record the discussion. After 10 minutes, the next student can ask their questions about their topic, and so on. When all members of the group have had their topic discussed and recorded, it is useful to give feedback to each other about how well the focus group interviews went:

- What worked well and not so well with each interview session?
- How could the interview questions have been improved?
- Were the questions leading in any way?
- Did the interviewer remain non-judgemental?
- Did the interviewer listen to the research participants' responses and probe appropriately?
- Did the interviewer check for meaning and clarification during the interview?

Practise listening to the recording, transcribing it and giving copies back to your friends to check on the contents. This is good practice for your ethical interviewing.

EMAIL AND SKYPE INTERVIEWS

As emails, discussion forums and Skyping are now ubiquitous, it is possible to interview respondents online. This works particularly well if a researcher has previously made face-to-face contact with the respondents and possibly discussed the research with them, but increasingly as people become more familiar with web-based meetings and discussions this is no longer the case. Skype interviews can be carried out just like a face-to-face interview but of course at a distance. Skype interviews can be efficient, time saving and a cheap way of getting interview data at convenience for both the respondent and the researcher.

Email interviews can then provide a follow-up to the initial discussion and allow the respondents further space to elaborate on their answers. It is also possible that the anonymity provided by the internet allows respondents to be more honest than in a face-to-face situation. Email interviews tend to be more like structured interviews with fixed questions that the respondent then answers, as in the following example. However, interviews can be carried out on social networking sites that can be more flexible.

EXAMPLE 9.1: EMAIL INTERVIEW

Hi John,

Last month when we met, you very kindly responded to some questions about the changing role of assessment in the early years. You provided some fascinating and exciting responses and I have analysed your responses on the attached sheet. As you can see, you made quite a lot of comments about the changing role of early years assessment. I wondered if I could ask you to possibly spare another five minutes of your precious time and briefly answer the following questions, please? You can just write your answers under the questions and email them back to me. That would be great! ☺

1.　Have the new forms of assessment affected you or your colleagues' pedagogy at all? If so, how?

If we are just looking at a final point, we end up missing so many goals that we never knew existed. I think that there is no doubt that if you have an idea of a fixed point that children in your care are going to have to reach to be seen as 'succeeding' (whether you agree with the criteria or not), it is going to be difficult to ignore it and go on as before. Of course, we all have high expectations and want our children to reach their potential. However, the shame of it is that, without directly saying it should, the curriculum's increased focus on academic subjects narrows and limits its reach, and as ever, the loser here is likely to be children's creativity.

2.　To what extent do you think the assessment changes might raise teachers' expectations and therefore standards?

What these changes seem to suggest to me is that despite having Communication and Language as a Prime Area, teachers are being forced to jump over this and prioritise things such as phonics, reading and writing. This might work for some children but for others they will be being asked to do things without the building blocks being properly in place. It's the same with Maths in that there is a real danger that a focus will be given to the more formal and sometimes abstract aspects of counting and calculating and not the more embodied aspects of mathematical understanding such as mass, area and height that come about through block play, trips to the park, games, etc. It seems to me that this greater focus on Maths and Literacy encourages a fencing off between curriculum areas rather than encouraging the cross-curricular principles that have been the bedrock of EY teaching for decades. Also, what happened to the idea that the different areas had equal status???

3.　Have you been encouraged to focus your attention on specific children so you get better results?

Actually, yes, we do higher up the school! But as a nursery teacher I am very glad not to have been put in this position. I think in our school, particularly in the early years, we are very good at focusing on the children and giving them what they need as individuals. However, with the older children the school does a lot of booster classes. There is very little creativity in the curriculum because of the huge pressure on getting good results. To me this seems much more focused on the school's reputation than preparing a child for their next steps in their learning and experience. It is not difficult at all to see a point in time where the government begins to exert a similar pressure for results of a particular kind in the early years. It would then be inevitable that this might lead to 'booster' classes in Reception and Nursery.

4.   What do the children make of the new forms of assessment?

I'll be honest, whenever I try to do something fancy and results-driven the children show me how uninteresting it is and before long we are doing something led by them that takes us to all sorts of places and new learning.

   Once again, many thanks for your time with this and see you soon.

All best wishes.

SUMMARY

This chapter has discussed:

- a range of different types of interviews with children and adults
- the skills and sensitivity that are needed to carry out focus group discussions with young children
- the ways in which children can act as co-researchers
- the ways in which structured activities can be used with young children whilst interviewing
- the importance of tape-recording interviews wherever possible.

RECOMMENDED READING

Folque, M. (2010) 'Interviewing young children', in G. MacNaughton, S. Rolfe and I. Siraj-Blatchford (eds), *Doing Early Childhood Research: International Perspectives on Theory and Practice*, 2nd edition. Buckingham: Open University Press. This thorough chapter contains a wealth of information on how to carry out ethically sound interviews with young children. It also details the ways in which the sampling process can occur through the description of a case study.

WEB LINKS

http://ro.uwe.ac.uk/RenderPages/RenderLearningObject.aspx?Context=7&Area=1&Room=3
&Constellation=25&LearningObject=120 – this website provides user-friendly advice with
tailor-made questions for designing your interview questions.

www.lse.ac.uk/media%40lse/research/EUKidsOnline/BestPracticeGuide/FAQ15.aspx – a useful
website detailing practical considerations for the best ways to interview children.

REFERENCE

Cave, K. (2011) *Something Else*. London: Penguin.

For additional online resources, please visit **https://study.sagepub.com/roberts-holmes4e**

10

ANALYSING YOUR QUALITATIVE AND QUANTITATIVE DATA FINDINGS

Now that you have your 'findings', or data, from your research project, it is time to make sense of all of these! This chapter explores the various ways in which you can interpret, understand and make sense of all the data you have gathered. This process is known as the analysis of data. Often in a research project, there will be a lot of data collected so it is vital that this information is carefully organised and presented so that an analysis can be carried out.

From the perspective of writing up your research project, your findings can be presented and analysed together in the same chapter or you can divide the findings and analysis over two different chapters. This chapter demonstrates how you can integrate your findings and analysis together as often the process of presenting your data will also involve its analysis.

REDUCING YOUR DATA

Your research project may have generated both qualitative and quantitative data in various forms – for example, questionnaires, interviews, observations, pictures and video, and from children and adults. So how do you make sense of and present this mass of data? Very often, it will not be possible to present *all* of your findings so you will have to select some. This process is known as *reducing* your data. The process involves generating key **codes** and themes from the data in the following way.

HOW TO REDUCE YOUR DATA

- Become really familiar and knowledgeable about the data you have collected by listening carefully to interviews and reading through transcriptions of all these and then re-reading them.
- Look out for patterns and similarities in the qualitative interviews and questionnaire quantitative data.
- These patterns or similar data can be coded together. This process of thematically

ordering and sorting your data is known as *coding*. You can work with both quantitative and qualitative data together.

- Coding helps you to see the patterns emerging from your data. You might find you have approximately six to ten main codes.
- Look carefully at all the codes you have generated. Which of these can be grouped together to form a theme? Now try to

subsume the different codes into perhaps four to six main themes or arguments. These themes will become your main arguments in the analysis and discussion.

- How do these themes answer your research questions?

- How are these themes related to the literature?
- Under each theme, discuss the data with the literature. This produces your discussion and analysis, as in Figure 10.1.

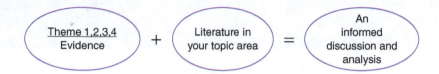

Figure 10.1 How themes discussed with literature produce a discussion

In his rough and tumble research project (case study 10.1), how does Mark identify the different codes? How many codes does he identify? How did he generate the themes?

── 🔍 ── CASE STUDY 10.1 ─────────────────

CODING AND THEMES IN A MIXED METHODS CASE STUDY

Coding was initiated by reading the questionnaires, transcribing the interviews and looking again at the videos. This continued with repeated re-reading of the data and included the noting down of ideas and evidence of patterns emerging. Codes were generated whereby phrases, sentences or whole paragraphs with similar 'events, realities, meanings and experiences' (Robson, 2016: 474) were marked in highlighter and coloured font. Subsequently, through a process of repeated re-reading of the transcripts, existing codes were either confirmed or reallocated and additional codes began to emerge. Surviving codes were developed and further refined through the process of correlating these findings with the literature. The final coding plan can be seen in Table 10.1.

Table 10.1 Codes and themes arising from interview transcripts and open questions from questionnaires

	Codes	Themes
1	Development and finding out	Defined through a sense of rough-and-tumbles (R&Ts) contribution to a child's development, learning and 'finding out' about themselves
2	A natural thing	This code describes R&T as an inherent and 'natural' drive within the developing child
3	Feel-good factor	R&T is defined as being an activity that gives pleasure and promotes well-being and connection

	Codes	Themes
4	Protection	Children are seen to be in need of protection from harm and more physically active and 'noisy' children
5	Safety and fear	Encompasses issues of safety, risk, hurt, fear, negative emotions, danger and injury
6	Space	Where space is seen as an implicated factor in the provision for, and quality of, R&T play
7	Personal experiences of gender	Instances of personal experiences of R&T in relation to speaker's gender
8	Gender	This code covers instances of comment or discussion on gender and difference from a generalised viewpoint
9	Boys and girls	Encompasses thoughts on what it is to be a boy or a girl in this particular setting in relation to R&T play
10	The engagement rules	Attitudes, policing, conventions, interventions, rules and restrictions
11	Power, adults and authority	This code is described by the power relationships that interact between parents, practitioners and state
12	Culture	Reflections on how culture impacts children with regard to R&T play

Table 10.2   Themes and their related codes and descriptors

Themes and related codes	Descriptors
'I can be myself' • Development and 'finding out' • A natural thing • The feel-good factor	This theme captured not only the many positive ways that the stakeholders felt that rough and tumble (R&T) can contribute to, and provide opportunities for, children's learning and development, but also the sense that it was a natural and inherent thing to do. There are many instances describing the positive affect generated by this style of play and the potential it has for generating well-being.
'Bruises and scrapes' • Protection • Safety and fear • Space	This theme is defined by the ways in which the various stakeholders express their concerns for the safety of the children. Space is particularly implicated in this. Issues and tensions around responsibility and protection are also the subject of this theme.
'That male/female thing' • Personal experiences of gender • Gender • Boys and girls	The over-arching topic of this theme is gender and the ways in which boys and girls are perceived to play and behave differently. It includes elements of personal and family experience as well as the impressions and understandings gained from stakeholders from witnessing the children in R&T play. There are also instances where participants' thinking around gender more generally is expressed.
'As long as they know the limits' • The engagement rules • Adults, power and authority • Culture	This theme is based on issues of power and the ways in which children and their play are contained and managed within the setting and at home. Rules and restrictions are set out, as are the effects of the intersecting power relations between parents, practitioners and the state. The theme also encapsulates ideas about culture and difference with regard to physically active play and gender in particular.

(Continued)

Having established the initial codes (in Table 10.1), these were then grouped together in themes that related to the research questions and the emerging arguments from the data. The codes and themes were then reviewed for consistency and coherency. Where necessary, some codes were either subsumed into others and reassigned under different themes or were renamed. Further analysis involved the generation and refining of a clear definition and name for the four themes. Themes were named using the words and phrases of the participants themselves, which allowed for authenticity and further levels of understanding and meaning to occur. The final themes, their defining characteristics and their related codes can be seen in Table 10.2. Finally, examples of data that particularly captured and shed light on each of the following themes were used to further analyse and explore the research questions and the related literature.

A CASE STUDY DEMONSTRATING THE IDENTIFICATION OF CODES AND DESCRIPTORS FROM AN INTERVIEW TRANSCRIPT

The short interview transcript from an outdoor research project, in case study 10.2, demonstrates the process of coding an interview. The different numbers were colour coded.

CASE STUDY 10.2

I think the fact that we ensure that come rain or shine (1) we take the children out everyday is really good news. We've always done that but now that the curriculum states (2) we should it is supportive and encouraging of what I believe in really. At this nursery, I have to say that we really like playing and working with the children in the outdoors here. I think this is partly because some of us went on a training course (3) and I have had a lot of outdoor-type experience myself when I was growing up (4) with my sisters (5). So, I feel really confident taking the children out and giving them outdoor experiences (4). We have a small back yard space (5) and covered area where we have sand and water play and a few wheelies. The boys in particular seem to benefit from being outdoors – they are always out there. We have to monitor that and see that the girls use it just as much (5). Although we don't have a big garden ourselves, there's a fantastic bit of woodland just round the corner from here. It's about 10 minutes walk away. The older children love going in there as it's like a natural wilderness (6). We have had campfires in there, being very careful of course (7), and sung songs around the fire. In the summer we have picnics in there together and the children love it and so do I! We go out there in the rain sometimes because we have a saying that there is no such thing as bad weather, only bad clothing! (6) Some of the parents don't like it though 'cos the children get a bit muddy and especially if they don't have boots and so on – that's really frustrating (8).

Possible emerging topic codes for case study 10.2 could be:

1. Weather not important.
2. Curriculum encouraging practitioners' beliefs.
3. Training giving confidence.
4. Autobiography supportive of outdoor play.
5. Gender and outdoor space.
6. Close to nature.
7. Health and safety issues.
8. Parental concerns.

Using these eight broad topic codes, it is now possible to go through all the other transcripts and identify those pieces of interview data and observations that might fit under these topic codes. These topic codes are then subsumed into broader and more general themes.

REDUCING AND DISPLAYING YOUR DATA

Generating your codes and themes from the data is the first part of data reduction. You are reducing the mass of observations and interviews into a few core key themes or 'headlines'. The second part of data reduction is to display those key themes or core ideas in tables and charts. Figure 10.2 outlines this process of data reduction and display. A convenient way to present your data in the findings chapter is to *reduce and display* these down into graphs, diagrams, tables and interview selections.

The themes that you have compiled can be displayed in tables. This process of reducing and displaying your data will further help you to understand the data and this makes analysis easier. Organising and sorting your themes into tables will certainly help you clarify the issues that arise from the data.

In our next example, an early years student is researching the extent to which different nurseries engage with outdoor play. The student has purposively sampled two nurseries that she knows have different ways of working outdoors with children. She has used questionnaires, interviews and observations to collect her data. She has gone through the steps outlined above and has compiled eight main themes from her questionnaires, interviews and observations. These main themes are presented in Table 10.3. The display helps to draw out the similarities and differences between each nursery.

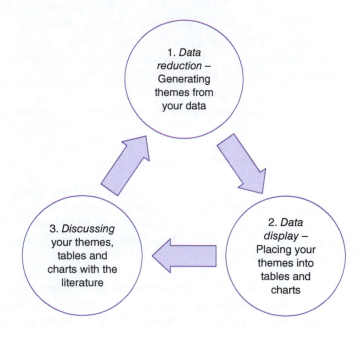

Figure 10.2 The relationship between data reduction, display and analysis

Table 10.3 Key outdoor play themes in two nurseries

Themes	Low Field Nursery	Spring Garden Nursery
1. Space	Lack of space - hard concrete area; overgrown bushes; mud	Large garden and field - range of grass, trees and bushes
2. Practitioners' training	Practitioners apprehensive about health and safety issues	Practitioners had all attended outdoor spaces workshop and feel confident outdoors
3. Clothing	Many children come in poor quality outdoor clothes	Parents are aware of providing children with good quality outdoor clothing
4. Gender issues	Girls reluctant to participate outdoors	Boys and girls enjoying the outdoors
5. Staff ratios	Insufficient staff hence outdoor ratios problematic	Sufficient staff to cover outdoor ratios
6. Resources	Few wheelies; dirty sandpit; broken furniture	Bikes, scooters, swings, slides, sandpit, large hill, climbing apparatus, outdoor water area
7. Context	Busy road next to nursery	Quiet area

ANALYSING YOUR DATA
QUANTITATIVE DATA ANALYSIS

Computer software such as Excel is an excellent way to help you organise, analyse and display your quantitative data. But it must be remembered that any software package is a tool for analysis – it cannot do this for you. In the outdoor research project in case study 10.2, the student made a questionnaire using the Likert scale and distributed it to 20 practitioners. She gave the same questionnaire to an equal number of practitioners in both Low Field Nursery and Spring Garden Nursery. Figures 10.3 and 10.4 show a compilation of the responses from the 20 questionnaires from each of the nurseries.

Within the Excel programme, the questionnaire data in Figures 10.3 and 10.4 can be transformed into graphs and the two data sets can then be compared (Figure 10.5). Web-based survey companies (discussed in Chapter 8) do such numerical data analysis and produce graphical representations, and this helps with the analysis of findings. It certainly demonstrates how the two nurseries utilise their outdoor space.

To what extent is the outdoor space utilised at Spring Garden Nursery?					
	Strongly Agree	Agree	Unsure	Disagree	Strongly Disagree
I am happy to work with the children outdoors	17		3		
I like the outdoor requirement in the EYFS	12	8			
We have enough staff to cover the ratios outdoors	10	5	5		
I have not attended outdoor training courses		1		3	16
The children come with adequate clothing	9	4	7		
The parents are unhappy when the children get wet		1	3	2	14
Both boys and girls spend the same amount of time outdoors	11	3	4	2	
There are insufficient resources for the outdoors			3	6	11
I want to spend more time outdoors	10	6	4		
Children need to be outdoors for long periods	14	3	2	1	

Figure 10.3 **Excel table of Spring Garden Nursery responses from 20 completed questionnaires**

To what extent is the outdoor space utilised at Low Field Nursery?					
	Strongly Agree	Agree	Unsure	Disagree	Strongly Disagree
I am happy to work with the children outdoors	11		7	2	
I like the outdoor requirement in the EYFS	5	3	12		
We have enough staff to cover the ratios outdoors			10	5	5
I have not attended outdoor training courses	17			3	
The children come with adequate clothing		4	7		9
The parents are unhappy when the children get wet	15	3		2	
Both boys and girls spend the same amount of time outdoors		3	12	5	
There are insufficient resources for the outdoors	14	3	3		
I want to spend more time outdoors	2	6	1	3	8
Children need to be outdoors for long periods	4		10	6	

Figure 10.4   **Excel table of Low Field Nursery responses from 20 completed questionnaires**

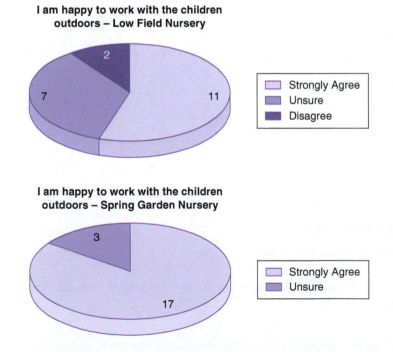

I am happy to work with the children outdoors – Low Field Nursery

- Strongly Agree
- Unsure
- Disagree

I am happy to work with the children outdoors – Spring Garden Nursery

- Strongly Agree
- Unsure

Figure 10.5   **Graphs generated in Excel from the data in Figures 10.3 and 10.4**

INDUCING AND/OR DEDUCING THE THEMES AND TOPIC CODES

When generating your themes or topic codes, it is possible to go directly up from the data, as in Figure 10.6.

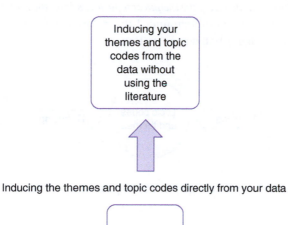

Inducing your themes and topic codes from the data without using the literature

Inducing the themes and topic codes directly from your data

Your data

Figure 10.6   **The themes being induced from the data**

In Figure 10.6, you will see that there are no pre-specified codes that you will impose on your data. You will simply let the data suggest the codes and themes. This **inductive** or bottom-up

Topic codes or themes from literature in your area and/or other similar projects

Deducing the themes and codes from the literature in your area

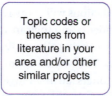

Your data

Figure 10.7   **The themes being deduced from the literature onto your data**

approach is also known as a **grounded theory** approach. On the other hand, the deductive analytical approach means that the researcher is working with pre-specified codes and themes that have already been decided on as important within the literature. The researcher then imposes these themes on the data. The themes might come directly from the literature or a similar research project to yours. Here, you will simply wish to import topic codes or themes into your project. This is known as *deducing the themes or topic areas from the literature* (see Figure 10.7). In reality, researchers often use both a grounded theory approach and a deductive approach based on the literature (as Figure 10.8 demonstrates).

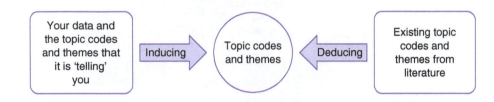

Figure 10.8   **The topic themes coming from both your data and the literature**

USING BOTH QUALITATIVE AND QUANTITATIVE DATA IN YOUR ANALYSIS

It is also important that your research tells the complexity of a story by using as wide a range of both qualitative and quantitative data as possible, possibly in a mixed methods study. Try to avoid using your data to make black and white arguments as early childhood issues are usually not polarised in such a simple way. Often, people and institutions will act in contradictory and sometimes incoherent ways. Practitioners and parents might say one thing about their practice with children but, when you observe them, do another. If possible, your research data should discuss such contradictions. These contradictions will show readers that your research has captured the complexities of the research respondents and their institutions.

If you can include a range of 'voices' offering alternative perspectives in your discussion, this will inevitably lead to such complexity. The Mosaic approach, discussed earlier, encourages the 'voices' of children, adults and practitioners. Such a range of 'voices' then encourages different perspectives on the same issue to emerge. Such a range of perspectives and ideas from various people makes the research more convincing. People experience early childhood institutions in different ways and hence the research would be unconvincing if all these different groups thought exactly the same way about the research issue. Different ways of seeing the same thing, and sometimes disagreements, can be healthy for an institution's development. Your research report should reflect any such differences.

Becoming familiar with the literature in your topic area will greatly assist you in the process of identifying the significant data you have collected. Being well versed in the literature is essential here, since you will be able, immediately, to spot issues arising from your data that are also discussed in that literature. First-time early childhood researchers are often unsure about which data to incorporate in their discussion and which to leave out. This process of matching up – and discussing, 'interrogating' and breaking down – what you found in the interviews, questionnaires and drawings, with what the literature says, is at the heart of a good discussion and analysis section. Hence, a good grasp of the literature in your topic area will be critical in helping you analyse your data successfully.

The fragments of data which are chosen will be 'rich' in the sense of containing key aspects of your developing argument. You must *tell* readers what you believe the data extract to be saying – what do you feel the data you have selected contribute to your arguments? Key to your discussion will be telling the story of why you used the data that you analysed.

There are several questions to ask yourself as you organise your data:

1. Why have I selected this particular piece of data?
2. What is it telling me?
3. How do the data I have chosen support my arguments?

It is important to state why you have chosen a particular piece of data. Choosing data is often to do with the construction of an argument or idea which you believe in and wish your study to highlight.

Knowing the literature in your field will help you recognise the different themes which emerge from the data. Themes will have often been sparked off in the researcher's mind throughout the entire research process. These then provide the headings for the discussion and stages in the argument.

ANALYSIS OF A MIXED METHODS CASE STUDY

In the mixed methods research project on gendered friendships (case study 10.3), notice how the qualitative and quantitative data are analysed and organised together under the different thematic headings and not the different research methods.

ACTIVITY 10.1

As you read case study 10.3, think about the following questions:

*   How are the three themes linked together?
*   What are the main arguments?
*   How do the arguments build on the data and the literature?
*   How are the data integrated with the literature?
*   What forms of data were used?
*   Are you convinced by the analysis and arguments?
*   Have you been provided with sufficient data to make your own judgements and interpretations?

── 🔍 ── CASE STUDY 10.3 ──────────

Theme 1: Friendship groups

The drawing, observational and interview data pointed towards a tendency for same-sex friendships. However, the data from these different sources could also be interpreted as showing that some children had mixed-gender friendship groups. Small groups of children, 22 in all, were asked to draw a picture of themselves playing with their friends. Each drawing was analysed by asking the following questions:

- What was the sex of the drawer?
- What were the sexes of the children drawn?
- What games did the drawing show?

The drawings produced some interesting quantitative and qualitative data: 60 per cent of the girls and 80 per cent of the boys drew children of their sex only. This finding may be graphically represented in the pie charts in Figures 10.9 and 10.10.

The data from the pie charts may be interpreted to suggest that there is clear evidence of a single-sex bias in the friendships of the Year 1 class. No claim is made for the statistical reliability of the findings since there were only 22 drawings made in the one classroom. This finding echoes previous research, which has noted sex-based friendships as a characteristic of children's peer relationships (Erwin, 1998; Jacklin and Lacey, 1997; Maccoby, 1996). The development of this same-sex friendship preference has been considered to run parallel with the development of gender identity itself (Erwin, 1998). At first sight, the drawing data would appear to confirm that children's understandings of what it means to be a boy or a girl within the cultural and social contexts of their worlds, lead them to establish and maintain relationships largely with same-sex peers.

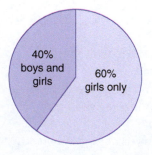

Figure 10.9   Sixty per cent of girls drew only other girls as their friends

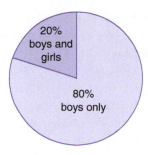

Figure 10.10   **Eighty per cent of boys drew only other boys as their friends**

However, the fact that 40 per cent of the girls drew girls and boys as being their friends and that 20 per cent of the boys included girls as their friends needs discussing (see Figure 10.11). That twice as many girls drew boys as their friends than boys drew girls as their friends suggests that it may be more acceptable for girls to play with boys than for boys to play with girls. That this interpretation may be made from this small-scale study is confirmed by Epstein (1998: 107), who has noted that 'for a girl, being more boyish means being more powerful in the world. For a boy to be more female is to be less powerful'. That 40 per cent of the girls chose boys amongst their friends but only 20 per cent of the boys chose girls as their friends confirms this assertion. This finding is also given support by Skelton (2001: 78), who claimed that it is rarer to see boys 'crossing over' the gender divide to play with girls than for girls to cross over and play with boys. Indeed, one of the girls interviewed was proud of playing mainly with boys: 'My Mum says I play with boys 'cos I'm a tomboy you see.'

Figure 10.11   **Chantel's picture showing both girls and boys as her friends**

(Continued)

Although Connor drew mainly girls in his picture and according to my observations often played with girls, he denied that he did so in a subsequent group interview. Connor's contradictory behaviour may perhaps be explained by Epstein's (1998) argument above that boys lose power within a patriarchal society by regularly playing with girls. Skelton (2001) noted that within a school context, boys who engage with feminine stereotypical play may make themselves vulnerable to teasing by other boys and girls. Thus, for boys to play with girls may be potentially problematic in that bullying of the boy may occur. Mac An Ghail (1994) noted that 'schools operate as masculine making devices', and Epstein (1998: 12) noted that schools are 'particularly difficult places for boys to depart from the norm'. That Connor denied that he played with girls may be because boys and girls actively 'police' each other's genders, thereby reinforcing stereotypical gendered behaviour (MacNaughton, 2000). Perhaps in the context of a group interview with other boys present, Connor would make himself too vulnerable if he said he mostly played with girls. On reflection, a group interview with Connor and some girls may have been a more appropriate context in which to interview Connor.

A content analysis of the children's play by sex confirms Craft's (1994) argument that children tend to hold stereotypical views about what it is appropriate for boys to play and what it is appropriate for girls to play. The boys overwhelmingly chose aggressive and competitive subjects to draw, such as dinosaurs, football and action men, whilst the girls chose to draw more gentle subjects, such as flowers, and opted for home-based activities such as playing with Barbie dolls and painting. My observations of the children in the playground confirmed that some boys were engaged in more physical activities than some girls. Such shared similar play interests serve to develop the relationships between the girls and between the boys respectively. They develop their separate interests and skills together, building on their expertise in these various activities.

The above arguments concerning the ways in which children 'police' each other's behaviour (Epstein, 1998; Mac An Ghail, 1994; Skelton, 2001) may have influenced the children's drawings. That the drawings were carried out by the children sitting together may have encouraged their stereotypical content. On reflection, perhaps the drawings should have been carried out individually, but ethically this may not have been appropriate.

The observations of the children both in the classroom and the playground, however, both confirmed and contradicted the above discussion. Observations showed that whilst some classroom behaviour confirmed some boys as demanding more of the teacher's time than the girls, other boys were quiet, shy and compliant in class. Girls and boys intermingled, chatted and shared work in the classroom:

(23.01.04, Literacy Hour Group Work, 9.45-10.45)

Anne, Jane, Jake, Stuart and Billy are making a shared book together based on 'Brown Bear Brown Bear'. There is much discussion between the children about the organisation and layout of their pictures and writing for their book. Jake and Jane are often seen to be laughing about humorous ideas for their book. They are enjoying each other's company.

This observation shows the way in which children within the classroom context may be socialised to work and play together (MacNaughton, 2000). However, in the different context of the playground the division between boys' and girls' friendship groups was more apparent:

(The following observation serves to illustrate some boys physically taking up space and knocking other boys, and girls in particular, out of the way.)

(28.01.04, Afternoon Playtime, 2.30–2.40)

Indoor/outdoor differences in friendship groups:

Jake, Ben and Danny are running around the playground, holding hands in a line. The boys are laughing and shouting about what good friends they are. They run around the playground with the line being broken and re-made as they crash into other children. Ben stops to have a drink from the water fountain. Danny pushes him out of the way in a friendly way and tries to get in front of Ben to have a drink himself. Ben pushes him back. 'Hey, what are you doing man?!!!' Ben shouts, laughing at the same time. Ben and Danny continue to push each other until the playground teacher tells them to stop and to use all their 'boisterous energy to play a game of football on the grass'.

The above example shows three boys engaging in an aggressive and dominating physical activity and confirming stereotypical gendered boys' behaviour. This finding confirms MacNaughton's (2000) view that boys are socialised to take up more playground space and dominate public spaces. The children's behaviour with their friends reflects the societal meanings that they have come to attach to the separate labels of 'boy' and 'girl'. Additionally, the teacher and thus the institution confirm the boys' gender and physical dominance by telling them to play football with their high energy levels. This finding confirms Craft's (1994) and MacNaughton's (2000) argument that the schooling process is central in confirming children's gender. But even here there was some mixing. Mostly boys and a handful of girls would play football, taking up a great deal of the playground space, whilst some boys and predominately girls played quietly round the edges with clapping games, talking, imaginative games, and games of 'It'. For example, Maria and Charlie enjoyed playing Spiderman together in the playground:

Charlie: We have this cool Spiderman game where Maria puts her pullover over her shoulders and says 'Spiderman' and then I chase her all over the place.

Maria: Yeah, he catches me sometimes then we swap round and he's Spiderman.

(Continued)

My observations showed that Charlie and Maria clearly enjoyed each other's company, both in the playground and in the classroom, thus questioning some of the findings which suggest the dominance of single-sex friendship groups. I interviewed the playground assistants and they confirmed my observations.

Theme 2: Gendered friendship qualities

Maccoby (1996) argues for the existence of gendered friendship qualities, and the data I collected in the drawings, observations and discussions concurred with this. Maccoby suggests that some boys will look for friendships associated with power and excitement. The predominance of football in the boys' drawings and other physical sports supported this view. However, Jake's comment below shows that, whilst boys are aware that being hard physical players and friends is generally a positive friendship attribute, they are also aware that aggressive physical force outside a game situation is to be avoided, as demonstrated at the end of the following interview with Jake, Lewis and Jane:

Researcher:	What do you think makes a good friend?
Jake:	I like a friend that is kind to me and helps me with my work and I like a friend that plays football with me. All the boys play football, Jack, Lewis …
Lewis:	Yeah, yeah, I like a friend that plays football with me and plays with me in the playground.
Jane:	I like a friend that plays with me. I like it when my friends come to my house for a party.
Lewis:	Yeah, I like a friend that comes by my house and plays with my remote controlled car.
Researcher:	So what do you think does not make a good friend?
Jane:	I don't like a friend who puts me down or is mean to me. I don't like a friend that bosses me about.
Jake:	I don't like a friend that hits me. You have to tell before they run to the teacher and tell a lie! Tell that you hit them!!! I don't like people who do that.
Lewis:	Billy isn't my friend when he loses at a game. He always loses and hits other people and then … and then hits me too. He shouldn't do that after we've finished football should he?

Here, activity, power and aggression are not characteristics that Jake or Lewis consider to be agreeable in a friend. The language they use mirrors the 'active, invasive, aggressive and bullying' descriptions of bad friends that the boys gave in Craft's (1994: 189) study. Therefore, it could be argued that, for some of the boys at least, stereotypical boys' behaviour is not regarded as a positive friendship attribute. Maccoby (1996) contends that girls look for their communal needs to be met through friendship and Jane certainly confirms this in the above interview. However, Jake also mentions above that he likes friends that are kind to him and help him with this work.

Maccoby (1996) believes girls view intimacy, love and communion as positive friendship attributes. Jane, above, confirms Maccoby's desired female friendship qualities. However, these were not qualities that were solely confined to the girls' friendship expectations. Concerning his picture (see Figure 10.12), William said that George was his friend because George 'helps me', 'is kind to me' and 'speaks nicely to me'.

Figure 10.12   **William and George playing football together**

The complexity of children's friendships was supported by the classroom teacher's response as to whether she believed the boys and girls in her class looked for different qualities in their friends: 'No ... no. I wouldn't say that. I think boys and girls look for the same things from friendship. They want somebody to play with, be nice to them and play good games ...'.

Jacklin and Lacey (1997) suggest that the impact that the teacher has on classroom relationships is important and may well set the tone for friendships within the classroom. They highlight the importance of a teacher and school intervention to assure equality and gender integration in early years settings.

The research question which guided this study asked what the relationship between gender and friendship was amongst young children. The study confirms MacNaughton's

(Continued)

(2000) work which points to how societal notions of gender-appropriate behaviour influence children's friendship groups. The research corroborates existing knowledge about peer relations, particularly concerning the qualities that young boys and girls associate with the notion of friendship. The study confirms the literature that suggests friendship is a vehicle that children use to explore their place in the world, and that their assumptions about the behaviour of boys and girls are reflected in the friendships they form.

SUMMARY

This chapter has:

- discussed the process for *reducing and displaying* your data
- shown how you can produce codes and themes
- explained how to produce an analysis based within the literature.

RECOMMENDED READING

MacNaughton, G. and Hughes, P. (2008) *Doing Action Research in Early Childhood Studies*. Buckingham: Open University Press. 'Step 12: Analyse your data' goes through the entire data process from start to finish. Clear steps are shown for how to code and present your data as well as how to sift through those data for patterns.

Richards, L. (2015) *Handling Qualitative Data: A Practical Guide*, 3rd edition. London: Sage. This book provides a very user-friendly overview of the whole process of analysing your data. It is packed full of diagrams and case studies which clearly explain the ways in which researchers analyse their data.

 ## WEB LINK

www.nfer.ac.uk/schools/developing-young-researchers/how-to-present-your-results – this website contains useful information on both qualitative and quantitative data analysis.

REFERENCES

Craft, A. (1994) Five and six year-olds' views of friendship, *Education Studies*, 20(2): 181–94.
Epstein, D. (1998) 'Real boys don't work', in D. Epstein, J. Elwood, V. Hey and J. Maw (eds), *Failing Boys? Issues in Gender and Achievement*. Buckingham: Open University Press.

Erwin, P. (1998) *Friendship in Childhood and Adolescence*. London: Routledge.

Jacklin, A. and Lacey, C. (1997) Gender integration in the infant classroom: a case study, *British Educational Research Journal*, 23(5): 623–39.

Mac an Ghail, M. (1994) *The Making of Men: Masculinities, Sexualities, and Schooling*. Buckingham: Open University Press.

Maccoby, E. (1996) 'Gender as a social category', in W. Bukowski, A. Newcomb and W. Hartup (eds), *The Company They Keep: Friendship in Childhood and Adolescence*. Cambridge: Cambridge University Press.

MacNaughton, G. (2000) *Rethinking Gender in Early Childhood*. London: Paul Chapman.

Robson (2016) *Real World Research*. Chichester: John Wiley & Sons Ltd.

Skelton, C. (2001) *Schooling the Boys: Masculinities and Primary Education*. Buckingham: Open University Press.

For additional online resources, please visit **https://study.sagepub.com/roberts-holmes4e**

WRITING UP
YOUR RESEARCH
PROJECT

STEPS BEFORE SUBMITTING YOUR RESEARCH PROJECT

Before you actually begin your data collection and fieldwork, there will be several steps to go through. The first important step is to choose your research area through a combination of both professional and personal interests combined with reflection on reading a wide range of literature. As you read, you will begin to think of research questions and these will evolve over time as you read even more! Also, as you read research articles you will begin to see a variety of research designs, methods and ethical issues in the literature which will prove helpful in developing your project. It is also vital to carefully follow your university's ethical procedure deadlines and processes. If your university has a date for the submission of ethical paperwork, make sure you know when this is and what is required. Remember, you will not be allowed to collect any data until your ethics paperwork has been approved! So, here is a checklist for you to work through as you plan your research project, with columns to note the date you started and completed this work.

TIMETABLING YOUR RESEARCH PROJECT

At the beginning of your research project, the submission deadline will probably seem a long way off, but it will quickly come around! So, in order to submit on time, one of the first things you must do is to work out a timetable for your research project as you must submit this work on time! It is a good idea to start by writing down the submission date and then working backwards from this (use Table 11.1 for this). Your planning can also be done using a downloadable Gantt chart, as suggested in the web links section at the end of this chapter.

Note that the various sections of the project are not written sequentially. So, for example, a survey of the literature is likely to be the first stage in your research project and therefore it would be logical to begin with a draft of the literature review. It is a really good idea to agree hand-in dates with your supervisor for your draft chapters and then you can carefully plan your diary to meet those dates. Table 11.2 shows a typical research project timetable.

Table 11.1　**Checklist before data collection**

Steps towards the fieldwork	Date started	Date done
Choosing a research area, and then a tighter research focus		
Reading existing research in this area and drafting an outline of the literature review		
Formulating research questions and then refining them		
Describing the methodology and selecting the methods		
Applying for and gaining ethical approval		
Designing and piloting the data collection techniques		
Selecting the sample and obtaining informed consent		
Starting the data collection		

Table 11.2　**A typical research project timetable**

Action	Month
Wide reading and note taking in the general topic area	Spring and summer months
Submit research plan	October
Define research questions and agree with supervisor	October
Apply for and gain ethical approval	October/November
Access research setting	November
Write ongoing literature review	November/December
Carry out fieldwork	November through to February
Analyse data	February/March
Write up project	February/March
Submit the research study	End of March

KEY QUESTIONS TO THINK ABOUT

Most of the information needed to answer the following key questions will be found in your course booklet. So make sure you have carefully read and understood that booklet, the dates and the course requirements! From that, try to answer the questions in Table 11.3.

Most undergraduate projects are approximately 6–10,000 words long, whilst a masters dissertation is more in the region of 15–20,000 words. One of the first questions that many students ask is how long each section should be. There is no fixed answer to this but Tables 11.4 and 11.5 show approximate guidelines and recommended lengths.

Table 11.3   Key questions

Questions	Answers
When is the submission deadline?	
What is the maximum number of words allowed for the research project? How many words am I allowed over and under this maximum number?	
How many chapters are expected and what are the chapter titles?	
How many words are expected in a typical chapter?	
Does my supervisor expect draft chapters to be written?	
When do I have to submit my ethics paperwork and when can I expect ethical approval?	
What paperwork is needed to gain ethical approval? Data collection sheet examples? Sample? Informed consent sheets? Information leaflets?	
Is a pilot study expected to check that the data collection methods are OK?	
When is the best time for data collection in the early years setting? When are the holidays? When are key members of staff available?	

Table 11.4   Recommended lengths for different sections of the research report expressed as percentages of total word count

Section	Percentage
Abstract	2.5%
Literature review	30% (Introduction 5% of this)
Methodology	17.5%
Findings	30%
Discussion	20%

Source: Wyse and Cowan (2017)

Table 11.5   Recommended lengths for different sections of a 6,000-word research report expressed as number of words

Section	Word total
Abstract	150
Literature review	1,800
Methodology	1,050
Findings	1,800
Discussion	1,200

SUPERVISION

YOUR SUPERVISOR

Your supervisor may have chosen you as one of their students because they have the necessary expertise, current knowledge and interest concerning your particular topic area. The professional and academic relationship between supervisor and student demands that both have certain duties, roles and responsibilities that they should perform. At the heart of the relationship will be a desire on the part of both supervisor and student to have the research project successfully completed on time.

Your supervisor has a number of responsibilities, including:

- giving advice about the suitability and appropriateness of your research topic
- commenting on the ethical dilemmas
- discussing suitable methods
- suggesting literature sources
- setting up a timetable of tutorials and listening to your questions, asking questions of you and advising you on the progress of your research study
- reading and commenting on your draft written work, possibly using 'track changes' and 'comments'.

YOUR RESPONSIBILITIES

Just as your supervisor has a number of responsibilities, so too do you. These may include the following:

- prioritising your attendance at supervision sessions
- identifying your interest area and reading and writing throughout the project at the appropriate level
- emailing work a few days in advance of tutorials so that your supervisor has sufficient time to read the work and make comments
- locating and making access arrangements to an early childhood setting in which to carry out your study
- listening to and acting on your supervisor's advice
- sticking to the agreed timetable to ensure submission by the deadline!

YOUR SUPERVISION MEETINGS

Clearly, your supervisor is crucial in ensuring that your research project is successful, so do make sure that you know exactly when you are meeting and what you are discussing at each meeting. It is important to maintain a good relationship with your supervisor so always be punctual and make sure you have emailed written work ahead of your meeting. If you are an international student, you might use Skype for your tutorial. Email written drafts to your tutor at least two or three days ahead of the meeting to give them sufficient time to make comments on your written work using 'track changes' and 'comments'. Make sure that you have done all the work they expected you to do from the previous meeting. It is always a good idea to have an emailed written record of your tutorial meeting so that both you and your supervisor are clear about what was said and about future action. Your university might have a supervision form similar to the boxed example.

EARLY CHILDHOOD RESEARCH PROJECT SUPERVISION FORM

Name of student:

Name of tutor:

Date and time:

Topic of research project:

Progress since last tutorial:

1.
2.
3.

Agreed action (to be completed by next meeting):

1.
2.
3.

Agreed date of next meeting:

Student signature/date:

Tutor signature/date:

CONTENTS OF YOUR RESEARCH PROJECT

Table 11.6 shows what the entire contents of a typical research project might contain. It is an excellent idea to confirm your university expectations by accessing past research projects in your library. Look carefully at their contents and learn exactly how these projects were organised and laid out. If there is none available in your university library, ask your supervisor whether you can take a look at one. A list of what your final research project or dissertation should include is laid out in Table 11.6, along with a checklist to tick when this is complete.

Table 11.6   Research project checklist

Section	Tick when completed
Title page: this should include your name, the year, your course, the institution and the total word length	
Acknowledgements: early years institution, family, friends, supervisor	
Abstract: very short (about 300 words) summary of entire project	
Table of contents: this should note the page numbers for all the chapters with their introductions and sub-headings and conclusions	
List of tables, figures and appendices with page numbers	
Introduction: a short rationale for the project; your personal and professional motivations; the research questions and an overview methodology	
Chapter 1: Literature review	
Chapter 2: Methodology	
Chapter 3: Findings	
Chapter 4: Discussion and conclusions	
References: ensure you are familiar with university expectations regarding style	
Appendices: ethical approval letters, informed consent forms, brief information on early years institution, sample questionnaire, sample transcript interview	

TITLE PAGE

It is a good idea to have a draft 'working title' throughout your study and then towards the end settle on your final title. A lack of focus on exactly what the research is about can be a common problem with some projects, so a draft working title clearly stating what the research is about will help you concentrate on this throughout the project. You can discover good titles by looking through research articles and former student research projects in your library. Often, a good title is short and to the point, clearly stating the topic area and the methodological approach, for example:

> *Assessment in the Early Years: Exploring Young Children's Rights and Participatory Practices through Action Research*

This student's title begins by clearly stating that the research focuses on assessment. After the colon, this is further explained – the research adopts a child-centred rights approach and uses action research methodology. Using a colon in this way is a common strategy for titles. Overall, this is a good title since it clearly articulates what the research project is about, its theoretical premise and its methodology.

Here is another successful (and actual) student project title:

> *'The Roly-Poly Stuff': An In-depth Case Study Examining Attitudes to, and Provision for, Rough and Tumble Play in the Nursery*

This title really stands out as it cleverly uses a short research respondent's quote which neatly captures the spirit of the study, and readers' attention! After the colon, the rest of the title succinctly states that the research is a case study focusing on rough and tumble play. This is a short and attractive title which again clearly hones in on what the research is all about. Don't forget to add your name, the course title and word count, and any other information your university requires on the title page.

ACKNOWLEDGEMENTS

The acknowledgements are often written on their own page. It is sometimes nice to simply dedicate, or acknowledge, your hard work to all the people who have helped you throughout the project, so you may wish to thank your family and friends for example, and probably the professional colleagues and children in the research institution who gave up the time for your study as well as your college supervisor.

ABSTRACT

The function of the abstract is to briefly summarise everything in your project in about 300 words. Hence, the abstract is usually written last! It is designed to help readers gain a rapid overview of your entire research project. It provides a complete overview of your research project by summarising all the main sections. Therefore, the abstract should succinctly state the aim of your research, its methodology and the main findings from your research report. It should tell readers about the context of your study and the questions asked, the theoretical framework you are drawing on, the research methodology and methods chosen with an indication of the main findings, and, if relevant, the implications for the early years.

SAMPLE ABSTRACT

Take a look at the following abstract which is from the student's research project entitled *Assessment in the Early Years: Exploring Young Children's Rights and Participatory Practices through Action Research.*

This research is a qualitative, action research case study which sets out to examine assessment practices in one nursery class in an inner city primary school. The study aimed to determine whether those assessment practices adequately captured the thoughts, feelings and experiences of quiet and silent children and those whose home language was not shared by others in that setting. The study reviewed the implications of the United Nations *Convention on the Rights of the Child* (1989) which promotes the rights of all children to self-expression, and contrasted that principle with the dominant discourse of 'school readiness' currently at play in the Statutory Framework for the Early Years Foundation Stage in England (DfE, 2012a: 2).

This has a clear identification of research methodology. And, again, a very clear sentence detailing exactly what the study set out to examine.

The study consulted practitioners during a focus group and showed that the downward pressure exerted by the demand to make all children ready for school resulted in practitioners feeling they weren't fully able to engage with children or parents to develop reciprocal relationships. The study used participatory methods drawn from the Mosaic approach (Clark and Moss, 2011), namely photography and book-making to support multi-modal communication by a small group of five children. Learning stories were written to demonstrate a credit-based assessment practice that could offer an alternative to the traditional methods used in the setting. This study concluded that while participatory methods of assessment such as the Mosaic approach (Clark and Moss, 2011) and learning stories (Carr, 2001) certainly helped to reveal the richness, joy and wonder of young children's lives, the curriculum itself, specifically the statements within Development Matters areas of learning and age bands (DfE, 2012b), was not able to fully reflect those attributes and instead devalued children's experiences.

In this paragraph, we are given more detail on the data collection methods. It is a short paragraph stating what the main findings were.

This abstract works well because it is clear, succinct and makes explicit the entire story of the research in three short paragraphs. The first two lines of the first paragraph contain a complete synopsis and state the central aim of the research. It then states that the methodology is action research and child-centred and provides a critical theoretical context for the research. The second paragraph states the research's participatory methodology, the research methods and the main findings from the project. Quite a feat in 275 words!

TABLE OF CONTENTS

The table of contents page provides a complete overview of all the research project's various chapters, sections and sub-headings along with their page number location within the entire project. The example in Figure 11.1 is taken from the early childhood education masters thesis whose title and abstract you have read above.

The first of the four chapters contains a short introduction to the project followed by the main literature review with seven separate sub-headings and a chapter summary. The second chapter on methodology has seven separate sub-headings (including methodology; validity; methods; setting; sampling; data analysis; and ethics). The third chapter is concerned with the findings from your research project and has five sub-headings based on the findings themes and a summary chapter. Finally, Chapter 4 is concerned with an academic discussion of the findings and conclusions from the research project and again is sub-divided into sections. Following these substantive chapters is a list of the references and then five separate appendices.

(Continued)

4.2 Competing discourses in the early years	69
4.3 Implications of the research	75
4.4 Limitations of the study	78
4.5 Recommendations for future research	78
4.6 Final comments	80
References	81
Appendices	86
Appendix 2.1: Focus group transcript	86
Appendix 2.2: Narrative observation template	96
Appendix 2.3: Learning stories	97
Appendix 2.4: Photograph coding	109
Appendix 2.5: Information sheets and informed consent forms	114

Figure 11.1 Research project contents page

CHAPTER 1: INTRODUCTION AND LITERATURE REVIEW

The first chapter within a research project is called the Introduction and Literature Review. This introduction is usually a short section which introduces the rationale for your study and sets the context, and due to its short length it does not warrant a separate chapter of its own. Hence, the introduction can be a separate section on its own or it can be contained as the beginning of Chapter 1. The main purpose of the introduction is to orient readers to your study. The section introduces your topic of study by clearly identifying the focus of inquiry and providing a background to your study. Along with the abstract, this introductory chapter is often the last chapter to be written as by then you will know and be able to present all the various aspects of your project.

SAMPLE INTRODUCTION

The following example is the introduction from a Chinese student's early years research project which examined Chinese teachers' attitudes towards play.

The rationale for the study is the researcher's own professional experience as an early years teacher in a state-funded kindergarten in China. I frequently experienced tensions between my belief in the importance and value of play and the lack of play in the practices taking place around me in the Chinese early years setting. This led to my interest in understanding how play is perceived by my colleagues and other Chinese early years teachers. By contrast in Western countries, where teachers frequently encourage play, research has shown that play contributes to children's overall development, and play has long been recognised and advocated as a vehicle for learning (Vong, 2012). Although attempts have been made by Western educationalists and theorists to define the notion of 'play', it remains a challenge as to what the term actually means and there is no consensus in existing research about what play is and what it is for (Fleer, 2009).

Always a good idea to include professional and personal reasons for the study. A strong confident opening paragraph setting out the theoretical boundaries.

A rationale for this study is to explore different constructions of play in three settings in China. Tobin, Wu and Davidson's (1989) comparative research on early years education in China, Japan and the United States discovers the powerful influence exercised by cultural values on the beliefs and practice of early years education. Due to the importance attached to early years education globally, the role and value of play, and the balance between play and learning, have become a central concern internationally **(Wu and Rao, 2008)**. Within the Chinese cultural context, the education of China has long been characterised by the stress for academic success and diligence (Vong, 2012). Many influential ancient Chinese educationists and theorists share the belief that little importance should be directed to play and that hard work is the only route to success (Wu and Rao, 2011). Play is defined in Chinese culture as indulging oneself in relaxation and joy, which is often associated with a negative connotation and regarded as divorced from learning (Liu, 2005). Although there is increasing awareness of the significance of play among Chinese early years teachers and scholars, Chinese teachers still find it challenging to encourage children to learn through play (Hua, 1998). Teachers are faced with constraints and impediments coming from social, philosophical and cultural beliefs, such as cultural values and parental expectations of education and social and economic factors such as the financial status of settings (Vong, 2012). Although some attempts have been made to investigate the implementation of play in early years education in China, research regarding play in China is still limited (Vong, 2012).

Good references throughout to both Chinese and Western literature sources. A very clear rationale for the study.

The study is framed by the following four research questions:

1. What are teachers' perceptions of the role and value of play in early years education in three Beijing early years settings?
2. What are the factors contributing to shaping teachers' perceptions of play?
3. What are the play opportunities provided for children in three different Beijing early years settings?
4. Which factors influence children's play opportunities in the settings?

This introduction to the research project is successful because the student has combined her personal and professional interests with a wide overview of the literature. She has clearly shown how her research builds on the limited research within the Chinese context and she has also outlined some of the key arguments for and differences between the European and Chinese cultural contexts. This section is then completed by outlining the four research questions.

LITERATURE REVIEW

The literature review is a very important part of a research project and therefore Chapter 3 is dedicated to this with examples. Suffice to note again here that the main purpose of the literature review is to identify what knowledge already exists about the area you are researching. The process of reading for and writing your literature review will help you learn more about the field you are investigating. Everything you write here must be directly relevant to your research in order that you will be able to refer back to some aspects of this chapter in the discussion and conclusion chapter. The literature review will situate your research within the existing field of knowledge and within current debates. Be sure to identify the various theoretical perspectives and methodological approaches taken by the authors you cite. You will also need to communicate how your study is related to existing theories in the field, and how you will frame your study theoretically.

CHAPTER 2: METHODOLOGY

Your second substantive chapter is the methodology chapter and in this you should restate your research questions and the central aim of your study. This chapter will include a clear description and justification of your research design and methods, clearly showing how the design will enable you to answer the research questions and how they are compatible with your theoretical framework. The following sub-headings should be included in your methodology chapter:

1. Research questions: clearly state the three, four or five main research questions that your research will answer.
2. Methodological approach: is your research qualitative, quantitative or mixed methods? How does your methodological approach help to answer your research questions? Clearly state the link and relationship between your research questions and your methodology.
3. Sampling: how have you chosen your research sample? Have you used a form of representative sampling or purposive sampling? Why have you chosen this form of sampling?
4. Data collection: clearly state what range of methods you actually used to collect your data and why you chose those particular methods. This section should also make reference to your pilot study and how that influenced the main study. A greater range and diversity of both **qualitative** and quantitative research methods generates greater validity of findings.
5. Fieldwork timetable: exporting your Gantt chart to clearly show what you did and when is a useful technique to demonstrate to your readers that you have completed all the research stages.
6. Analysis: clearly state how you analysed your research findings. Researchers often use both an inductive grounded theory approach and deductive approaches from the research literature on your topic area.

7. Validity: how have you ensured validity of your findings? Have you used a mixed methods approach that has triangulated both qualitative and quantitative research methods? Have you ensured that you have a diversity of respondents? Have you included a reflective section about your particular philosophical and political approach, e.g. child-centred, feminist and/or anti-racist? Such reflexivity can help mitigate your bias.

8. Ethics: clearly state the ethical processes that you followed to collect your data. How has your project heard children's marginal 'voices' and those of practitioners, teachers and parents? How did you ensure informed consent was granted and did you gain this from the children?

A SMALL SECTION FROM A METHODOLOGY CHAPTER

The following small section of a student's methodology chapter has been chosen to exemplify the way in which that individual wrote a short introduction to their chapter which provides a good summary overview of the rest of the chapter. Writing a short introduction to each of your four chapters makes it easier for readers to understand the contents and line of argument of that chapter. This methodology introduction also re-states the research questions. The chapter then proceeds to explore the action research methodology with a useful diagram. Such diagrams and tables are helpful in explaining how the research was carried out.

2.1 INTRODUCTION

This piece of research is based on a case study approach that employed a small-scale, mixed methods, action research design. It set out to explore the attitudes of children, parents and practitioners to the rough and tumble (R&T) play of children attending the nursery class of an inner-city, grant-maintained primary school in East London. The questions that the study sought to explore were as follows:

1. What are the factors that determine the nature, frequency and uptake of R&T in children attending this nursery?

2. What are the attitudes and perceptions of children, parents and practitioners in relation to R&T, and do these impact on children's ability and willingness to engage in this play?

3. Is there anything about our pedagogy that we can change that would better provide for all children in this area?

The initial phase comprised a small-scale, mixed methods case study using both an interpretivist paradigm and empirical data to understand the attitudes to, provision for and nature of rough and tumble play within the setting. This included both questionnaires and semi-structured interviews. **Interpretivism** is defined by its focus on the understanding of multiple perspectives through a co-construction of reality by the researcher and participants (Robson, 2016). The findings of this initial research informed a second phase that included three intervention sessions (see below). Videoed observations during the third intervention and the subsequent interviews with children provided rich data with which to inform and explore future provision for R&T within the nursery and possibly future stages of this research.

2.2 RESEARCH DESIGN

Action research as an approach has been particularly popular in education, with its collaborative nature suiting flexible design approaches very well (Robson, 2016). It is predicated on the fundamental principal of research improving action (see Figure 1) and requires a depth of inquiry far greater than just practitioner reflexivity and the 'learning from experience' that this might initially imply (Baumfield et al., 2011). It requires more of a scientific rigour connected to a dialogue within a community of enquirers that links the students' learning with that of the practitioners (Dewey, 1910, cited in Baumfield et al., 2011). This collaboration is for some researchers the primary component in that it is only through working with and alongside others that an individual is supported into new thinking (Kemmis and McTaggart, 1988, cited in MacNaughton and Hughes, 2008). Thus, in different ways the research design sought to involve as much of the nursery community as was possible, including the children attending the nursery, the parents of those children, and the practitioners who worked there.

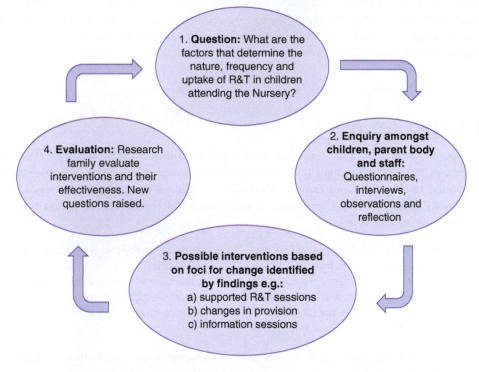

Figure 11.2   The action research cycle

Source: MacNaughton and Hughes (2008)

One of the important sub-sections within your methodology chapter should be concerned with how you analysed the data you collected.

CHAPTER 3: FINDINGS

In the findings chapter, you should present the most significant data and outcomes from your project. Your analysis will have led to the selection and rejection of some of your data. The chapter must not be simple description so should, for example, be presented in themes that have come from your analysis. It is therefore a good idea to begin the process of data analysis while you are still collecting the data. Over time, your analysis will build a framework for you to make comparisons across your data, and to understand and explain your findings. If you wish to, you can present your findings in a variety of ways such as tables, charts and diagrams. It will be clear to readers that the themes you chose for your findings in this chapter link with the theoretical ideas presented in your literature review, but in this chapter you do not have to cite the academic literature; you must merely present the data.

A SMALL SECTION OF A FINDINGS CHAPTER

The following example is taken from the rough and tumble research project and shows how the questionnaire data were presented as graphs and the interview data in themes. Only a few graphs and one theme out of seven themes are presented here. Notice how the interview data are located within their codes and then placed into the wider themes.

THE PRACTITIONER QUESTIONNAIRE

Figure 2 (a) shows that whereas in the nursery five of six practitioners perceive boys to be play-fighting at least two to four times per week, in Reception all seven practitioners perceive their boys to be rough and tumbling as little as weekly or less. As Figure 2 (b) shows, the figures for girls are less, with four out of six of those in Nursery and five of the seven Reception practitioners suggesting girls rough and tumble once a month or less.

Figure 3 (a) and (b) show the results for perceived play-fighting in the outside areas for both genders: (a) shows that the majority of both Reception and Nursery practitioners perceive that the boys play-fight outside two to four times per week or more in the case of the Nursery. Conversely, in (b) we see that the majority of practitioners in both year groups perceive that girls play-fight outside monthly or less.

INTERVIEWS

THEME 1 - I CAN BE MYSELF

This theme captures the ways in which the participants perceive rough and tumble play to be an expression of the natural child. Repeatedly, in both questionnaires and interviews, the early years practitioners referred to the varied developmental benefits of this type of play. The codes that comprise this theme are: Development and 'Finding out'; A Natural Thing; The Feel-Good Factor.

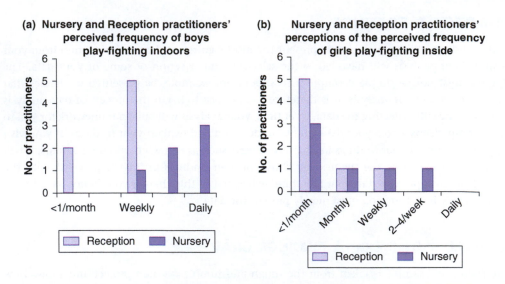

Figure 11.3 (a) and (b)   Practitioner questionnaire graphs: boys and girls play-fighting indoors

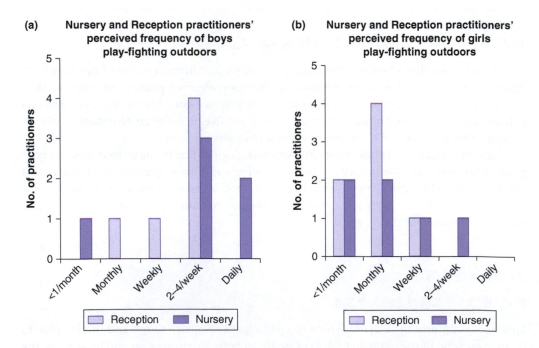

Figure 11.4 (a) and (b)   Graphs showing boys and girls play-fighting outdoors

DEVELOPMENT AND 'FINDING OUT'

The words 'develop' and 'development' occur frequently throughout the data and at least once in every item of script, whether it be from the questionnaires, focus group or interviews. Rough and tumble is seen by participants as a locus of opportunity for development in many of the key areas of the EYFS curriculum:

> 'Though it is only a little chunk it permeates through everything.' (Anna)

During their interviews, both Anna and Lesia directly mentioned different areas and strands of the EY curriculum that are supported by R&T, including:

> 'communication', 'PSE' and 'physical'. (Anna)

> 'physical development' and 'gross motor skills'. (Lesia)

One parent whose son engages daily in superhero play states:

> 'I truly believe that my son's language has developed because of the ability to pretend play.' (Parent 3)

The merits of R&T play are further expressed in the nursery staff focus group discussion:

> 'This is what the children need to help their development and imagination'. (Practitioner 4)

A key element in this theme is the agency with which children lead their learning through R&T play. This is expressed in:

> 'I think that children are going to be acting out and finding out about themselves'. (Anna)

This is also expressed in an answer to a question asking whether R&T should happen at school or in the home. One practitioner suggested that children should be:

> 'Working with children their own age to experiment with different ways of physicality'. (Practitioner 13)

A NATURAL THING

Rough and tumble is expressed as an inherent and irrepressible pastime for children by many of the participants:

> 'It's just a natural thing that they want to do anyway so it's like fighting a losing battle if you don't do it'. (Anna)

Phrases in Anna's interview such as *'muck about'*, *'flinging yourself through the air'* and *'clambering over things'* suggest a freedom, expansiveness and abandon to this kind of activity that are also hinted at in the language of others. When reminiscing about her own experiences of rough and tumbling as a child, Lesia remarks:

'I thought that that's how it was. That's how I liked it ... I can be myself'. (Lesia)

It suggests in Lesia an early belief that rough and tumble was part of childhood, part of life.

This sense that rough and tumble, for some, is just a natural part of children's lives was not restricted to these two women alone. For example, two other female practitioners stated:

'Two lively brothers - lots of chasing/playfighting at home'. (Practitioner 8)

'It was, strangely perhaps, part of "family tradition" most Sunday nights ... I loved it'. (Practitioner 9)

CHAPTER 4: DISCUSSION AND CONCLUSIONS

This chapter should begin with a clear statement of the most significant findings from your research as a whole. In this chapter, you can interrogate your findings with the literature that you have discussed in your literature review. This theoretical discussion might be organised according to the themes that emerged from your data. The discussion of the data should use the relevant literature already presented in your literature review and may also include new literature. In the conclusion, it is important that you acknowledge that you have not provided *all* the answers for your topic area, so you will need to acknowledge that your research is small-scale and cannot provide generalisations beyond the context of the research itself. The following questions may help you when thinking about this chapter:

- What were the main findings from your study?
- What have you found out from your study?
- How do your findings fit in with what is already known from the literature?
- Do they confirm and/or build on existing knowledge and understandings?

- What implications do they have for your professional practice?
- What further research could result from your work?
- How would you have modified your methodology to improve the validity of your results, a section that is often called 'limitations'?

A SMALL SECTION OF A DISCUSSION AND CONCLUSION CHAPTER

In the rough and tumble research project, this chapter used the following sub-headings: Introduction; Summary of Findings: Theoretical Framework; Gender; Space and Safety; Power and Authority; Development, Nature and the 'Feel-Good' Factor; Reflecting on the Research Questions; Limitations of the Project; and Concluding Comments. Here is a small extract of the discussion from one section showing how the researcher weaved together both theory and data into an academic discussion in which the literature supports and builds on the data.

The work of researchers into the ways in which children 'construct' (Paechter, 2006) and 'perform' (Butler, 2006) their genders resonates well with some of the discourses emerging from the data, as does the notion of 'communities of practice' of Paechter (2007). Comments such as, 'Girls mostly participate in home corner, play dough or painting whereas boys are more active and rough in their play' (Practitioner 4) and girls 'prefer to dress up and play in pretend role play' (Practitioner 6) are examples of markers within the shared repertoire of characteristics and behaviours that define being a girl or boy in the Nursery (Martin, 2011). Through the repetition of these discourses and the implied 'rightness' of these characteristics in the eyes of those in power (in this case the adults), these markers come to be seen as truths, thus reinforcing the behaviours and choices of both genders and maintaining gender boundaries as expressed in the borderwork of Thorne (1993).

In another section in this chapter called 'Reflecting on the Research Questions', Mark restated each of the three research questions and answered them. This is a good idea as it focuses the discussion back on the research questions. Here is one of the research questions with its answer.

Research Question 1: What are the factors that determine the nature, frequency and uptake of R&T by children attending this nursery?

A key theme that arose within both questionnaires and interviews was that of child safety. Parents and practitioners referred to the lack of physical space for this kind of activity both at home and at school and the fear of physical harm. Practitioners were particularly concerned about the harshness of the outside space and a culture of fear was apparent around allegations from parents of a lack of appropriate care for their children and even abuse. The balancing of some children's need to be physically active against those who might be alarmed or disturbed by such play was also a factor. The appropriateness of inter-gender touch was also suggested as a reason why girls in the school might be less predisposed to engage in R&T. It was these factors that appeared to drive 'the engagement rules' that policed and delimited R&T play in both Nursery and Reception classes. These rules placed very particular limits on where and how R&T play was allowed, with a range of sanctions that enforced them.

A further section that can go into this chapter, or the methods chapter, is concerned with the limitations of the study.

REFLECTING ON THE STUDY: ITS LIMITATIONS

The limited voice offered to the children in the initial stage of the study and then during the interventions has, it could be argued, diminished its reach within this particular phase. It is suggested that any successive cycle or study might explore in much greater depth the attitudes and beliefs of children to R&T play and include within this children with no interest in it. This would necessarily involve their greater participation in the raising of research questions and enabling them to play a more active part in the data generating process. More crucially, it would require young children contributing to and being consulted about any changes being made that affect their lives. This might be facilitated through the use of multi-modal methods such as the Mosaic approach.

Finally, this chapter has a 'concluding comments' sub-section which combines lines of argument on the data and theoretical perspectives.

CONCLUDING COMMENTS

This study has shed light on the many contradictions that exist within an inner-city nursery in relation to the rough and tumble play of its youngest stakeholders, the children. These have included highlighting the show of care by boys towards each other whilst play-fighting, despite the perception of its link to aggression. Also apparent is the resilience and independence in problem solving that both genders are capable of when given the right opportunity. However, prime among these contradictions has been the willingness and enthusiasm for R&T among girls, who are otherwise perceived by practitioners as having little interest in it. What is notable is that the girls' evident enjoyment is mirrored by that of practitioners' memories of their own R&T experiences when children themselves. This suggests the possibility that R&T should be as readily accepted as a play choice for girls as it is for boys and as readily available to them. Using concepts such as 'borders' (Thorne, 1993), 'communities of practice' (Paechter, 2007) and 'performative acts' (Butler, 2006), poststructuralist feminists have illustrated how children and adults can perpetuate inequalities and marginalise diversity. However, they have also encouraged the use of alternative strategies that promote the agency and voice of young children and offer opportunities for the challenging and transformation of societal and cultural discourses that would otherwise maintain the status quo.

REFERENCES

Correctly using citations and references is important because you must acknowledge those academics who you have read and used in your research report. Therefore, it is vital that you follow your own institution's rules to the letter regarding the details of how to present citations and references. The referencing process basically consists of two parts. First, there is the citation and this is included as part of a sentence in your research project text by stating the author's surname and year of publication of their text, for example (Roberts-Holmes, 2012). This may or may not include a direct quote. It should be noted that using too many direct quotes is a sign of weak writing. Second, there is the entry of this person's name into the reference list itself at the end of your research report. Here is an annotated example from the rough and tumble research reference list. The particular referencing system used here is known as the Harvard System.

BOOKS

Baumfield, V., Hall, E. and Wall, K. (2012) *Action Research in Education: Learning through Practitioner Enquiry*, 2nd edition. London: Sage.
Bryman, A. (2002) *Biographical Research*. Buckingham: Open University Press

BOOK CHAPTERS

Bitou, A. and Waller, T. (2011) 'Researching the rights of children under three years old to participate in the curriculum in early years education and care', in D. Harcourt, B. Perry and T. Waller (eds), *Researching Young Children's Perspectives* (pp. 52–67). London: Sage.
Brooker, L. (2005) 'Learning to be a child: cultural diversity and early childhood ideologies', in N. Yelland (ed.), *Critical Issues in Early Childhood* (pp. 115–30). Buckingham: Open University Press.

JOURNAL ARTICLES

Bradbury, A. (2011) 'Rethinking assessment and inequality: the production of disparities in attainment in early years education', *Journal of Education Policy*, 26(5): 655–76.
Braun, V. and Clarke, V. (2006) 'Using thematic analysis in psychology', *Qualitative Research in Psychology*, 3(2): 77–101.

WEB REFERENCES

British Educational Research Association (BERA) (2011) Ethical Guidelines for Educational Research. Available at: www.bera.ac.uk/publications/pdfs/ETHICAL (accessed 3 March 2013).

GOVERNMENT DOCUMENTS

Department for Children, Schools and Families (DCSF) (2007) *The Early Years Foundation Stage*. Nottingham: DCSF Publications.
Department for Children, Schools and Families (DCSF) (2008) *Practice Guidance for the Early Years Foundation Stage*. Nottingham: DCSF Publications.

APPENDICES

Within the appendices, you can place copies of children's pictures, questionnaire examples, interview transcriptions, the ethics forms, and information about the early childhood institution. Hence, your appendices might include some of the following: ethical approval letters; informed consent forms; brief information on the early years institution; sample questionnaire; sample transcript interview. Each appendix must be numbered.

PLAGIARISM

If you are under a time pressure, you may be tempted to try to pretend that someone else's work is your own. Presenting someone else's work, words or ideas as being your own can sometimes happen inadvertently by failing to attribute ideas or words to the person who wrote them. This pretence is known as plagiarism and is treated as a serious academic offence. Within the academic world, it is equivalent to stealing another person's work and if you are caught it is possible that you may fail your research project. With the now ubiquitous use of the internet, it is increasingly easy to mistakenly copy and paste another's work and then pretend it is your own. University tutors are usually quick to spot plagiarism and additionally all your written work now goes through electronic plagiarism checks when uploaded, so it is very likely that this will be spotted. So it is much better to write your own work than to get caught out!

FINAL PREPARATION AND PROOFREADING

All pages, after the title page, should be numbered in sequence. Numbering subheadings isn't absolutely necessary as it can result in less attention being paid to the coherence between sections, but then again it can be useful for cross-referencing within the dissertation. Bullet points are not normally used on the contents page. You should proofread your work before submission which basically means going very carefully through your writing, making sure that all the grammar, spellings, citations and references are correct. Does each sentence and paragraph make sense and are they appropriately connected? If possible, find someone who will proofread your work before you submit it to your supervisor. If English is an Additional Language (EAL) or you are an international student, you might need to secure the services of a professional proofreader and your supervisor will advise you on this. The main issue to remember with a proofreader is that they will take time, possibly two to three weeks, so do make sure you have timetabled for a proofreader if you require one!

Your supervisor will comment on your draft chapters, and may wish to see the complete dissertation before you prepare to submit it. Reading the complete work will take some time, and so you must allow your supervisor plenty of time to read it, and yourself sufficient time to respond to any comments. Before handing in your final draft to the supervisor, check through the following points:

- What is the main story here? Why is it interesting/relevant to early years?
- Is the structure of my research project clear so that readers can follow the story?
- Is my research project written so readers can clearly follow the lines of argument presented?
- Have I given enough detail about the context in which my research took place?
- Does the evidence presented fully support the claims I am making?
- Have I answered all my key research questions?
- Have I been clear about the boundaries of my research?

- Have I made clear why I decided to investigate my research questions, and have I justified my choice of research methodology and methods?
- In the final chapter, have I included my reflection on what I might have done better with hindsight, namely what worked well and what not so well?
- Have I suggested areas of research which might be worth further investigation?
- Are all the references included and have I consistently used the correct style as recommended by my university?

In planning the final stages of your submission, identify several days for printing and photocopying, and if necessary taking your work to a binder and collecting it before the submission date. Make sure you know how to upload your e-version to the university system and check whether this needs to be in the form of a Word document or a pdf.

CONGRATULATIONS!

Once you have submitted your research project, you should congratulate yourself! Your hard work and determination in getting to this point have furthered your knowledge about yourself and the topic area in which you have been so passionately interested. It is very likely that your research interest will continue into your work with young children and in turn this may well lead to enhanced job prospects. Many successful students state that their confidence rises once they have gained a qualification such as a degree, and they then apply for a promotion and during the interview they often end up talking about their research! The in-depth knowledge and understanding that their research project has given them can make them impressive at interviews. Making your research public within your university at seminars or at work in a staff meeting is a worthwhile endeavour for your personal development. If you have carried out your research within an early childhood institution, you can suggest that you feed back your findings at a staff meeting. You may also provide a summary sheet of your research conclusions. Before making such a presentation, talk through what you will say and write with your supervisor in order to ensure that whatever you say is ethically sensitive and insightful. The professionals who work in the institution will know better than you the constraints and limitations under which they work. You will need to think carefully about how your research can build on current practice in the institution. Early childhood research is a rapidly expanding area and you may wish to publish your research on a website or in a magazine, which is a great idea! Talk this through with your supervisor who may be able to assist you with this.

SUMMARY

This chapter has:

- examined how to write a convincing critical argument
- given you an overview of the organisation and structure of your project
- reflected on how to successfully use library resources for your literature review
- raised your awareness of how to structure and write a literature review
- helped you appreciate the dangers of plagiarism
- shown you how to correctly reference your literature sources.

RECOMMENDED READING

Punch, K. and Oancea, A. (2015) *Introduction to Research Methods in Education*, 2nd edition. London: Sage. This thorough research methods textbook provides an easy-to-use guide to the whole process of research writing. It also includes advice on structuring and organising your research outline.

Wyse, D. and Cowan, K. (2017) *The Good Writing Guide for Education Students*, 4th edition. London: Sage. This excellent student-focused book has chapters on referencing, grammar, punctuation, presentation, proofreading, and learning from feedback, which are all extremely useful in developing your writing.

WEB LINK

www2.le.ac.uk/offices/ld/resources/dissertations/getting-started/your-time-management/gantt-charts – this website has a downloadable Gantt timeline chart for planning your research project over time. Amending the Excel spreadsheet for your early childhood research project with deadlines and timelines will ensure you complete it on time.

REFERENCES

Baumfield, V., Hall, E. and Wall, K. (2012) *Action Research in Education: Learning through Practitioner Enquiry*, 2nd edition. London: Sage.

Butler, J. (2006) *Gender Trouble: Feminism and the Subversion of Identity*. London: Routledge.

MacNaughton, G. and Hughes, P. (2008) *Doing Action Research in Early Childhood Studies*. Maidenhead: Open University Press.

Paechter (2006) 'Masculine femininities/feminine masculinities: power, identities and gender', *Gender and Education*, 18 (3): 253–63.

Paechter (2007) *Being Boys; Being Girls: Learning Masculinities and Femininities: Learning masculinities and femininities*. London: McGraw-Hill Education.

Robson, C. (2016) *Real World Research*. Chichester: John Wiley & Sons Ltd.

Thorne, B. (1993) *Gender Play: Girls and Boys in School*. Buckingham: Open University Press.

Wyse. D. and Cowan, K. (2017) *The Good Writing Guide for Education Students* 4th edition. London: Sage.

For additional online resources, please visit **https://study.sagepub.com/roberts-holmes4e**

INDEX

Page numbers followed by 'f' denotes a figure and 't' denotes a table